75 Easy Paleo Slow Cooker Recipes

A Complete Paleo Plan for Your Entire Family

Disclaimer

No part of this eBook can be transmitted or reproduced in any form including print, electronic, photocopying, scanning, mechanical or recording without prior written permission from the author.

While the author has taken utmost efforts to ensure the accuracy of the written content, all readers are advised to follow information mentioned herein at their own risk. The author cannot be held responsible for any personal or commercial damage caused by misinterpretation of information. All readers are encouraged to seek professional advice when needed.

What You Will Find In This Book?

Paleo fully read as Paleolithic diet consist of food items that belong to the Paleolithic era. The fact that this diet belongs to the cavemen era does not mean that it is difficult to make and do not satisfy our taste buds.

As a matter of fact, Paleo food is very easy to make with most of the ingredients already available in the kitchen pantry. It is also very delicious and satisfies the contemporary taste provided you follow the right recipe.

This is where this book intervenes. It tells you around 75 amazing slow cooker Paleo recipes. Kids, teenagers, youngsters, adults and old age, this book have delectable Paleo recipes for all age groups and all mealtimes. The best thing about this book is that it tells you slow cooker recipes also known as the crock pot recipes. Now you don't have to stand by the stove all the time, the slow cooker recipes allows you to cook unattended.

Keep on reading and find a way to live a healthy and yummilicious Paleo lifestyle.

Why Paleo?

Paleo food is not just easy to make and tastes delicious, it provides innumerable health benefits. The latter advantage of Paleo is worth any and all efforts that you might have to go through to get used to the new lifestyle.

Nothing is worth your health. And with Paleo recipes, leading a healthy lifestyle is as easy as eating a hamburger. Paleo is extremely beneficial for people having sinus, high cholesterol, weak metabolism and depression.

Moreover, what makes Paleo attractive is that it has recipes for all age groups and mealtimes. Whether it is breakfast, lunch, snack time, appetizer or dinner, Paleo has a delicious meal for every occasion.

So just go ahead and try a few. A try is definitely worth the innumerable benefits Paleo offers.

Contents

Disclaimer 2
What You Will Find In This Book? 3
Why Paleo? 4
Paleo Slow Cooker Chicken Recipes 17
    Paleo Slow Cooker Spicy Lime Chicken 17
        Serving Size 17
        Nutritional Facts (Values per Serving) 17
        Ingredients 17
        Preparation Method 17
    Paleo Crock Pot Chicken Rolls 19
        Serving Size 19
        Nutritional Facts (Values per Serving) 19
        Ingredients 19
        Preparation Method 19
    Paleo Slow Cooker Chicken Curry 20
        Serving Size 20
        Nutritional Facts (Values per Serving) 20
        Ingredients 20
        Preparation Method 20
    Slow Cooker Spicy Chicken Verde with Sweet Nutty Squash 22
        Serving Size 22
        Nutritional Facts (Values per Serving) 22
        Ingredients 22
        Preparation Method 22
    Paleo Hot and Sweet Wings 24
        Serving Size 24
        Nutritional Facts (Values per Serving) 24
        Ingredients 24
        Preparation Method 24
    Crock Pot Chinese Chicken Wraps 26
        Serving Size 26
        Nutritional Facts (Values per Serving) 26
        Ingredients 26

  Preparation Method 26
 Crock Pot Asian Wings 28
  Serving Size 28
  Nutritional Facts (Values per Serving) 28
  Ingredients 28
  Preparation Method 28
 Crock Pot Garlic Chicken 30
  Serving Size 30
  Nutritional Facts (Values per Serving) 30
  Ingredients 30
  Preparation Method 30
 Slow Cooker Chicken Stew 32
  Serving Size 32
  Nutritional Facts (Values per Serving) 32
  Ingredients 32
  Preparation Method 33
 Sweet Dip Sesame Chicken 34
  Serving Size 34
  Nutritional Facts (Values per Serving) 34
  Ingredients 34
  Preparation Method 34
 Slow Cooker Buffalo Drumsticks 36
  Serving Size 36
  Nutritional Facts (Values per Serving) 36
  Ingredients 36
  Preparation Method 36
 Crock Pot Paleo Almond Chicken 37
  Serving Size 37
  Nutritional Facts (Values per Serving) 37
  Ingredients 37
  Preparation Method 37
 Slow Cooker Coconut Chicken 38
  Serving Size 38
  Nutritional Facts (Values per Serving) 38

- Ingredients 38
- Preparation Method 38

Crock Pot Jamaican Wings 39
- Serving Size 39
- Nutritional Facts (Values per Serving) 39
- Ingredients 39
- Preparation Method 39

Slow Cooker BBQ Chicken 41
- Serving Size 41
- Nutritional Facts (Values per Serving) 41
- Ingredients 41
- Preparation Method 41

Paleo Crock Pot Pulled Chicken with Spicy Sauce 43
- Serving Size 43
- Nutritional Facts (Values per Serving) 43
- Ingredients 43
- Preparation Method 43

Crock Pot Indian Chicken Curry 45
- Serving Size 45
- Nutritional Facts (Values per Serving) 45
- Ingredients 45
- Marinade Ingredients 45
- Preparation Method 46

Crock Pot Thai Noodles 48
- Serving Size 48
- Nutritional Facts (Values per Serving) 48
- Ingredients 48
- Preparation Method 49

Crock Pot Chicken Cacciatora 50
- Serving Size 50
- Nutritional Facts (Values per Serving) 50
- Ingredients 50
- Preparation Method 50

Slow Cooker Spicy Cilantro Wings 52

- Serving Size 52
- Nutritional Facts (Values per Serving) 52
- Ingredients 52
- Preparation Method 52
- Smoked Crock Pot Meatloaf 54
  - Serving Size 54
  - Nutritional Facts (Values per Serving) 54
  - Ingredients 54
  - Ingredients for the Sauce 54
  - Preparation Method 55

Paleo Slow Cooker Beef Recipes 56

- Paleo Beef Tacos 56
  - Serving Size 56
  - Nutritional Facts (Values per Serving) 56
  - Ingredients 56
  - Preparation Method 56
- Paleo Beef and Mushroom Meatloaf 58
  - Serving Size 58
  - Nutritional Facts (Values per Serving) 58
  - Ingredients 58
  - Preparation Method 58
- Slow Cooker Sweet Potato Casserole 60
  - Serving Size 60
  - Nutritional Facts (Values per Serving) 60
  - Ingredients 60
  - Spices 60
  - Preparation Method 60
- Slow Cooker Beefy Stew 62
  - Serving Size 62
  - Nutritional Facts (Values per Serving) 62
  - Ingredients 62
  - Preparation Method 63
- Slow Cooker Tongue with Red Sauce 64
  - Serving Size 64

- Nutritional Facts (Values per Serving) 64
- Ingredients 64
- Ingredients for the Sauce 64
- Preparation Method 65

Paleo Rib Beef N Bacon Burgers 66
- Serving Size 66
- Nutritional Facts (Values per Serving) 66
- Ingredients 66
- Preparation Method 66

Paleo Slow Cooker Pork Recipes 68

Crock Pot Pork Waffle Bars 68
- Serving Size 68
- Nutritional Facts (Values per Serving) 68
- Ingredients 68
- Ingredients for the Waffles 68
- Ingredients for the Mayo Sauce 69
- Preparation Method 69

Caramelized Pork Treat 71
- Serving Size 71
- Nutritional Facts (Values per Serving) 71
- Ingredients 71
- Preparation Method 71

Paleo Sausage Pie 73
- Serving Size 73
- Nutritional Facts (Values per Serving) 73
- Ingredients 73
- Preparation Method 73

Apple and Ginger Pork 75
- Serving Size 75
- Nutritional Facts (Values per Serving) 75
- Ingredients 75
- Preparation Method 75

Green Slow Cooker Pork 77
- Serving Size 77

- Nutritional Facts (Values per Serving) 77
- Ingredients 77
- Preparation Method 78
- Paleo Pork and Butternut Stew 79
  - Serving Size 79
  - Nutritional Facts (Values per Serving) 79
  - Ingredients 79
  - Preparation Method 79
- Crock Pot Pork Honey Ribs 81
  - Serving Size 81
  - Nutritional Facts (Values per Serving) 81
  - Ingredients 81
  - Preparation Method 81

Paleo Slow Cooker Mix Meat Treats 83

- Paleo Crock Pot Supreme Pizza 83
  - Serving Size 83
  - Nutritional Facts (Values per Serving) 83
  - Ingredients 83
  - Preparation Method 83
- Crock Pot Pine Nut Meatballs 85
  - Serving Size 85
  - Nutritional Facts (Values per Serving) 85
  - Ingredients 85
  - Preparation Method 85
- Paleo Mexican Rice 87
  - Serving Size 87
  - Nutritional Facts (Values per Serving) 87
  - Ingredients 87
  - Preparation Method 87
- Slow Cooker Meaty Stuff 89
  - Serving Size 89
  - Nutritional Facts (Values per Serving) 89
  - Ingredients 89
  - Preparation Method 89

Slow Cooker Meat Lovers 91
    Serving Size 91
    Nutritional Facts (Values per Serving) 91
    Ingredients 91
    Preparation Method 91

Smokey Crock Pot Pulled Pork 93
    Serving Size 93
    Nutritional Facts (Values per Serving) 93
    Ingredients 93
    Spices 93
    Preparation Method 93

Slow Cooker Chicken and Eggplant Lasagna 95
    Serving Size 95
    Nutritional Facts (Values per Serving) 95
    Ingredients 95
    Preparation Method 95

Slow Cooker Italian Treat 97
    Serving Size 97
    Nutritional Facts (Values per Serving) 97
    Ingredients 97
    Spices 97
    Preparation Method 98

Paleo BBQ Flavored Coffee Roast 99
    Serving Size 99
    Nutritional Facts (Values per Serving) 99
    Ingredients 99
    Seasonings 99
    Preparation Method 99

Slow Cooker Mexican Carnitas 101
    Serving Size 101
    Nutritional Facts (Values per Serving) 101
    Ingredients 101
    Preparation Method 102

Slow Cooker Meatballs 103

Serving Size 103

Nutritional Facts (Values per Serving) 103

Ingredients for Meatballs 103

Ingredients for Sauce 103

Preparation Method 104

Celebration Ribs 105

Serving Size 105

Nutritional Facts (Values per Serving) 105

Ingredients... 105

Preparation Method 106

Slow Cooker Paleo Chicken Stuffed Peppers 107

Serving Size 107

Nutritional Facts (Values per Serving) 107

Ingredients... 107

Preparation Method 107

Paleo Italian Shrimp Marinara 109

Serving Size 109

Nutritional Facts (Values per Serving) 109

Ingredients... 109

Preparation Method 109

Meat 'n' Chili 111

Serving Size 111

Nutritional Facts (Values per Serving) 111

Ingredients... 111

Preparation Method 112

Slow Cooker Jambalaya Stew 113

Serving Size 113

Nutritional Facts (Values per Serving) 113

Ingredients... 113

Preparation Method 113

Crockpot Sweet Butter 115

Serving Size 115

Nutritional Facts (Values per Serving) 115

Ingredients... 115

- Preparation Method 115
- Crock Pot Short Rib Tacos 117
  - Serving Size 117
  - Nutritional Facts (Values per Serving) 117
  - Ingredients 117
  - Ingredients for Tortillas 117
  - Preparation Method 117
- Stuffed Peppers Delight 119
  - Serving Size 119
  - Nutritional Facts (Values per Serving) 119
  - Ingredients 119
  - Preparation Method 119
- Hawaiian Paleo Salad 121
  - Serving Size 121
  - Nutritional Facts (Values per Serving) 121
  - Ingredients 121
  - Preparation Method 121
- Sweet Blueberry Carnitas 123
  - Serving Size 123
  - Nutritional Facts (Values per Serving) 123
  - Ingredients 123
  - Preparation Method 123
- Slow Cooker Sweet Potato Soup 125
  - Serving Size 125
  - Nutritional Facts (Values per Serving) 125
  - Ingredients 125
  - Preparation Method 125
- Paleo Detox Apples 126
  - Serving Size 126
  - Nutritional Facts (Values per Serving) 126
  - Ingredients 126
  - Preparation Method 126
- Asian Style Ribs 128
  - Serving Size 128

- Nutritional Facts (Values per Serving) 128
- Ingredients 128
- Preparation Method 128

Slow Cooker Barbacoa 130
- Serving Size 130
- Nutritional Facts (Values per Serving) 130
- Ingredients for Roast 130
- Ingredients for Sauce 130
- Preparation Method 131

Spicy Coffee Short Ribs 132
- Serving Size 132
- Nutritional Facts (Values per Serving) 132
- Ingredients 132
- Preparation Method 132

Crockpot Chicken Gravy 134
- Serving Size 134
- Nutritional Facts (Values per Serving) 134
- Ingredients 134
- Preparation Method 134

Paleo Ropa Vieja with Rice 136
- Serving Size 136
- Nutritional Facts (Values per Serving) 136
- Ingredients for Vieja 136
- Ingredients for rice 137
- Preparation Method 137

Crock Pot Roast with Mushroom Gravy 138
- Serving Size 138
- Nutritional Facts (Values per Serving) 138
- Ingredients 138
- Preparation Method 138

Slow Cooked Garlic Rump Roast 140
- Serving Size 140
- Nutritional Facts (Values per Serving) 140
- Ingredients 140

- Preparation Method 140
- Mexican Lime Soup with Rice 142
  - Serving Size 142
  - Nutritional Facts (Values per Serving) 142
  - Ingredients for Soup 142
  - Ingredients for Rice 142
  - Preparation Method 143
- Cinnamon Chops with Butternut Squash 144
  - Serving Size 144
  - Nutritional Facts (Values per Serving) 144
  - Ingredients 144
  - Ingredients for Butternut Squash 144
  - Preparation Method 145
- Slow Cooker Chuck Roast 147
  - Serving Size 147
  - Nutritional Facts (Values per Serving) 147
  - Ingredients 147
  - Preparation Method 147
- Paleo Chick 'n' Basil 148
  - Serving Size 148
  - Nutritional Facts (Values per Serving) 148
  - Ingredients 148
  - Preparation Method 148
- Paleo BBQ Style Bison 150
  - Serving Size 150
  - Nutritional Facts (Values per Serving) 150
  - Ingredients 150
  - Preparation Method 150
- Paleo Italian Roast with Balsamic Vinegar 152
  - Serving Size 152
  - Nutritional Facts (Values per Serving) 152
  - Ingredients 152
  - Spices 152
  - Preparation Method 152

- Slow Cooker Meat Fajitas 154
  - Serving Size 154
  - Nutritional Facts (Values per Serving) 154
  - Ingredients 154
  - Spices 154
  - Preparation Method 155
- Sweet and Hearty Lasagna 156
  - Serving Size 156
  - Nutritional Facts (Values per Serving) 156
  - Ingredients 156
  - Ingredients for Sauce 156
  - Preparation Method 157
- Crockpot Saffron Meat 158
  - Serving Size 158
  - Nutritional Facts (Values per Serving) 158
  - Ingredients 158
  - Spices 158
  - Ingredients for Sauce 159
  - Preparation Method 159
- Smokey Pork with BBQ Sauce 160
  - Serving Size 160
  - Nutritional Facts (Values per Serving) 160
  - Ingredients for BBQ Spice Blend 160
  - Ingredients for Sweet BBQ Sauce 161
  - Ingredients for Pork 161
  - Preparation Method 161
- Vegan Minestrone Soup 163
  - Serving Size 163
  - Nutritional Facts (Values per Serving) 163
  - Ingredients 163
  - Preparation Method 164

Final Words 165

Paleo Slow Cooker Chicken Recipes

Paleo Slow Cooker Spicy Lime Chicken

Serving Size

8 – 10 servings

Nutritional Facts (Values per Serving)

Calories/serving: 275

Total Carbohydrate: 9 g

Sodium: 976 mg

Protein: 45 g

Cholesterol: 117 mg

Total Fat: 4.7 g

Ingredients

1 whole chicken (organic) approx 6 lbs

1 tablespoon olive oil

1 teaspoon black pepper

1 teaspoon ground cumin

1 teaspoon sea salt

1 tablespoon red chili powder

1 tablespoon cayenne powder

1 cup of fresh cilantro

Half cup lime juice

1 whole lime for stuffing

3 cloves garlic

Preparation Method

1. Wash and dry the chicken with paper towels.

2. Dust the whole chicken with salt and pepper.
3. Apply a coat of cayenne powder, chili powder and cumin powder on it.
4. Take the whole lime and use a fork to poke holes in it.
5. Now sprinkle some chili powder on it and stuff it in the cavity of the chicken.
6. Blend cilantro, garlic, lime juice and olive oil thoroughly in a blender.
7. Put the chicken in large slow cooker liner and pour the blended mixture on top of it.
8. Make sure you marinate the chicken thoroughly. Use your hand to apply the mixture around the chicken and even under the skin.
9. Now pull the slow cooker liner tight around the chicken.
10. Let the chicken marinade overnight.
11. In the morning, put the chicken in a large slow cooker (at least 6 quarts).
12. Cook it on low heat for 6 – 8 hours.

The delectable Paleo Slow Cooker Spicy Lime Chicken is ready to serve.

Paleo Crock Pot Chicken Rolls

Serving Size

3 – 4 servings

Nutritional Facts (Values per Serving)

Calories/serving: 520

Total Carbohydrate: 28.8 g

Sodium: 1170 mg

Protein: 37 g

Cholesterol: 97 mg

Total Fat: 33 g

Ingredients

4 boneless chicken breasts

1 medium sized bunch of asparagus

8 slices of Prosciutto

8 Garlic cloves

Salt to taste

Black pepper to taste

Preparation Method

1. Slice the chicken breasts in half.

2. Hammer the chicken with a meat mallet. Smash it on both sides till it is thin enough to roll.

3. Roll the chicken around 3 pieces of asparagus and a chopped clove of garlic. Trim the asparagus to fit in the chicken roll.

4. Now roll of slice of Prosciutto around the rolled chicken.

5. Place all the rolls in a slow cooker and cook on low heat for 4 hours.

Serve with tomato ketchup. Enjoy!

Paleo Slow Cooker Chicken Curry

Serving Size

2 – 3 servings

Nutritional Facts (Values per Serving)

Calories/serving: 263.8

Total Carbohydrate: 12.8 g

Sodium: 405 mg

Protein: 30.7 g

Cholesterol: 65.7 mg

Total Fat: 10.3 g

Ingredients

1.5 lbs boneless chicken

2 cans of coconut milk

3 tablespoon Paleo curry paste

1 medium sized red bell pepper

1 medium sized green bell pepper

1 yellow onion

1 small cabbage

Preparation Method

1. Cut the boneless chicken in 1 inch cubes.
2. Cut the red and green bell peppers in about 1 inch cubes.
3. In a crock pot, stir well the curry paste and coconut milk.
4. Add the chicken cubes in it and stir well.
5. Now add the bell pepper cubes in the pot and stir well.
6. Slice the yellow onion and mix it in the pot with other ingredients.

7. Finally, grate the cabbage and stir it well in the crock pot.//
8. Now cover the pot and let it cook on low heat for 4 to 5 hours.
9. Garnish with red chili sauce.

Slow Cooker Spicy Chicken Verde with Sweet Nutty Squash

Serving Size

3 – 4 servings

Nutritional Facts (Values per Serving)

Calories/serving: 311

Total Carbohydrate: 32.2 g

Protein: 24.7 g

Cholesterol: 67 mg

Total Fat: 10.9 g

Ingredients

1 lb ground chicken

1 lb tomatillos (chopped)

1 tablespoon coconut oil

1 medium sized white onion (diced)

1 butternut squash (peeled and diced)

2 cans of diced green chilies

2 teaspoon cayenne powder

1 teaspoon garlic powder

1 teaspoon paprika

Preparation Method

1. Heat the coconut oil in a skillet over medium heat
2. Add cayenne powder, garlic powder in it.
3. Now add the ground chicken meat and butternut squash in the skillet.
4. Stir occasionally until the squash becomes soft and meat takes on a brown color.
5. Now add the diced onion in it and stir it well.

6. Remove the skillet from the heat and set it aside.
7. Line a crock pot with chopped tomatillos and canned chilies.
8. Put the skillet in the crock pot on top of the lined tomatillos and canned chilies.
9. Let it cook on low heat for 4 hours.

The delicious Slow Cooker Spicy Chicken Verde with Sweet Nutty Squash is ready to serve.

Paleo Hot and Sweet Wings

Serving Size

4 – 5 servings

Nutritional Facts (Values per Serving)

Calories/serving: 385

Total Carbohydrate: 57 g

Sodium: 1604 mg

Protein: 14 g

Total Fat: 17 g

Ingredients

4 lbs pastured chicken wings

1 cup beef stock

2 cups crushed pineapple

1 cup fresh mango puree

1 tablespoon coconut oil

4 cloves garlic (chopped)

2 jalapeno peppers (chopped)

1 habanero pepper (chopped)

2 teaspoons paprika

2 teaspoons cayenne pepper

6 ounce canned tomato paste

2 tablespoons apple cider vinegar

Half cup coconut milk

Preparation Method

1. To make the hot and sweet sauce, heat coconut oil in a pan over medium heat.

2. Add crushed garlic, jalapeno and habanero peppers in the oil and stir for about 5 minutes.

3. Add the mango puree and pineapple in the pan and stir for another 8 - 10 minutes.

4. Now add in it the beef stock, tomato paste, apple cider vinegar, paprika and cayenne pepper.

5. Reduce the heat to low and cover the pan.

6. Let it cook for 1 hour while stirring occasionally.

7. After an hour, turn off the heat and let the sauce cool slightly.

8. Blend it in a food processor to make a consistent thick sauce. Set aside the sauce and let's work on the chicken now.

9. Preheat the oven at 400°F.

10. Line a baking sheet with aluminum foil.

11. Set the wings on the tray such that one does not overlap the other.

12. Put this tray in the preheated oven for 10 minutes, or till the wings take on light brown color. Flip in between to bake the wings from both sides.

13. Now line a crock pot with half of the baked wings.

14. Top it with half of the hot and sweet sauce.

15. Now line the remaining wings in the pot and spread the remaining sauce on top of them.

16. Let the wings cook on low heat for 5 hours.

The appetizing Paleo Hot and Sweet Wings are ready to be enjoyed.

Crock Pot Chinese Chicken Wraps

Serving Size

4 – 5 servings

Nutritional Facts (Values per Serving)

Calories/serving: 393

Total Carbohydrate: 31 g

Sodium: 469 mg

Protein: 36 g

Cholesterol: 92 mg

Total Fat: 15 g

Ingredients

3 lbs pastured chicken thighs

1 medium sized red onion (thickly sliced)

1 tablespoon coconut oil

1 large bunch Collard Greens (At least one leaf to wrap one thigh and a few extra)

1 cup hot Chinese mustard

2 teaspoons cayenne pepper powder

1 teaspoon crushed red pepper

Garlic cloves equal to the number of thighs

Preparation Method

1. Heat coconut oil in a skillet over medium-high heat.

2. Stir chicken in it for about 5 minutes or till it becomes light brown.

3. Now wet the collard greens and microwave them for 1 minute. Don't overheat them. The purpose here is just to soften them enough to wrap the chicken.

4. In a bowl, mix well the Chinese mustard, sliced garlic cloves, crushed red pepper and cayenne pepper.

5. Coat the chicken thighs in the mustard paste and place it in center of the collard leaf.

6. Put an onion slice on top of the chicken and wrap the leaf around it.

7. Now grease the crock pot with coconut oil and line it up with a few collard leaves.

8. Place the wraps in the pot.

9. Once all the wraps are placed in the pot, cover them with a few collard leaves.

10. Let it cook on low heat for 6 hours.

Serve with tomato ketchup.

Crock Pot Asian Wings

Serving Size

5 – 6 servings

Nutritional Facts (Values per Serving)

Calories/serving: 60

Total Carbohydrate: 4 g

Sodium: 160 mg

Protein: 6 g

Cholesterol: 25 mg

Total Fat: 5 g

Ingredients

4 lbs pastured chicken wings

1 tablespoon coconut oil

Half cup coconut aminos

2 cloves garlic

1 tablespoon ginger powder

1 tablespoon apple cider vinegar

2 tablespoon hot sauce

1 tablespoon raw honey

Toasted sesame seeds to garnish

Preparation Method

1. Heat coconut oil in a skillet over medium-high heat.
2. Stir chicken in it for about 5 minutes or till it becomes light brown.
3. In a food processor, add coconut aminos, ginger powder, apple cider vinegar, hot sauce and raw honey. Blend all the ingredients well to make a consistent sauce.

4. Put the chicken wings in a slow cooker and top them up with the sauce.

5. Let it cook on low heat for 4 hours.

Garnish with toasted sesame seeds.

Crock Pot Garlic Chicken

Serving Size

Serves 4

Nutritional Facts (Values per Serving)

Calories/serving: 429

Total Carbohydrate: 11.2 g

Sodium: 534.5 mg

Protein: 31.8 g

Cholesterol: 131 mg

Total Fat: 28.3 g

Ingredients

1 whole chicken

1 small bunch of fresh thyme

Few sprigs of sage and fresh marjoram

Half lemon

40 cloves garlic

1 teaspoon paprika

Sea Salt to taste

Black pepper to taste

Preparation Method

1. Rinse and dry the chicken. Remove the excess fat pockets.
2. Peel the garlic cloves and line them in the crock pot.
3. Place the whole chicken, breast side up, in the pot on top of the garlic cloves.
4. Stuff the half cut lemon in the chicken cavity.
5. Sprinkle the paprika, salt and black pepper on the chicken.

6. Roughly tear off the thymes, sage and marjoram leaves and sprinkle them on the chicken.

7. Let it cook on low heat for 8 hours.

8. After 8 hours slow cooking, turn off the heat and carefully strip the chicken in individual pieces such as wings, leg and breast piece etcetera.

9. Line the chicken pieces on a baking tray and broil them for a few minutes or until the chicken skin becomes light crispy.

Serve with tomato ketchup. Enjoy!

Slow Cooker Chicken Stew

Serving Size

2 – 3 servings

Nutritional Facts (Values per Serving)

Calories/serving: 265

Total Carbohydrate: 12.8 g

Sodium: 542 mg

Protein: 34.0 g

Cholesterol: 85.3 mg

Total Fat: 5.2 g

Ingredients

2 lbs chicken breasts

2 tablespoons coconut oil

7 ounces tomato sauce

14 ounces diced tomatoes

1 medium sized green bell pepper (chopped)

1 medium sized yellow onion (chopped)

4 ounces canned jalapenos (chopped)

4 ounces canned green chilies (chopped)

2 teaspoons dried oregano

3 cloves garlic (minced)

1 tablespoon cumin powder

1 tablespoon chili powder

Sea salt to taste

Black pepper to taste

Cilantro leaves to garnish

Preparation Method

1. Add the chicken breasts in a slow cooker.
2. Now add all the remaining ingredients and spices in it.
3. Let it cook over low heat for 8 to 10 hours.
4. Garnish with cilantro and serve it hot.

Sweet Dip Sesame Chicken

Serving Size

2 – 3 servings

Nutritional Facts (Values per Serving)

Calories/serving: 509

Total Carbohydrate: 80.4 g

Sodium: 1377 mg

Protein: 29.6 g

Cholesterol: 75.5 mg

Total Fat: 9.9 g

Ingredients

3 lbs boneless and skinless chicken

2 cups honey

Half cup tomato ketchup

1 cup soy sauce

1 cup diced onion

Half teaspoon crushed red pepper

2 tablespoons olive oil

8 teaspoons corn starch

6 chopped scallions

2 cloves garlic (minced)

1 tablespoon Sesame seeds

Sea salt to taste

Black pepper to taste

Preparation Method

1. Season the chicken thoroughly with salt and pepper.
2. Put it in a slow cooker.
3. In a bowl, mix well the diced onions, soy sauce, olive oil, tomato ketchup, honey, minced garlic and crushed red pepper.
4. Pour this mixture in the slow cooker on top of the chicken.
5. Cover the pot and let it cook on low heat for 4 hours.
6. After 4 hours, carefully take the chicken out of the slow cooker. Let the sauce be in there.
7. Shred the chicken roughly in 1 inch pieces and set it aside.
8. In another bowl, dissolve the corn flour in 12 tablespoons distilled water.
9. Pour it in the slow cooker and stir it well with the sauce.
10. Replace the lid and let the sauce cook on high heat for another 10 minutes.
11. In a large serving bowl, spread the chicken pieces and pour the sauce on top of it.
12. Sprinkle the sesame seeds on top of it.

Garnish with chopped scallions.

Slow Cooker Buffalo Drumsticks

Serving Size

4 – 5 servings

Nutritional Facts (Values per Serving)

Calories/serving: 180

Total Carbohydrate: 4.0 g

Sodium: 1231 mg

Protein: 14.1 g

Cholesterol: 75 mg

Total Fat: 11 g

Ingredients

4 lbs chicken drumsticks

1 tablespoon coconut oil

4 ounces grass fed butter (substitute: 1/3 cup coconut oil)

1 cup Frank's Red Hot sauce

Preparation Method

1. Heat coconut oil in a skillet over medium-high heat.
2. Stir chicken in it for about 5 minutes or till it becomes light brown.
3. Melt the grass fed butter in a pan.
4. Add half cup hot sauce in the pan and mix it well with the butter.
5. Put the drumsticks in a crock pot and pour the butter sauce on top of it.
6. Use your hands to apply the butter marinade thoroughly on the drumsticks.
7. Top it up with the remaining red hot sauce.
8. Let it cook on low heat for 4 hours.

Serve with tomato ketchup. Enjoy!

Crock Pot Paleo Almond Chicken

Serving Size

2 – 3 servings

Nutritional Facts (Values per Serving)

Calories/serving: 251

Total Carbohydrate: 11 g

Sodium: 502 mg

Protein: 24 g

Cholesterol: 71 mg

Total Fat: 12 g

Ingredients

2 lbs boneless chicken breasts

Half cup chicken broth

Half cup almond butter

1 lemon

1 tablespoon cumin powder

1 teaspoon crushed garlic

¼ cup soy sauce

Preparation Method

1. Put the chicken breasts and almond butter in a slow cooker.
2. Stir in cumin and crushed garlic.
3. Squeeze in lemon, soy sauce and chicken broth in it.
4. Stir all the ingredients well.
5. Cover the pot and let it cook on low heat for 8 hours.

Serve with cooked cauliflower rice.

Slow Cooker Coconut Chicken

Serving Size

Serves 2

Nutritional Facts (Values per Serving)

Calories/serving: 376

Total Carbohydrate: 9.1 g

Sodium: 229 mg

Protein: 41.7 g

Cholesterol: 121 mg

Total Fat: 19.5 g

Ingredients

1 lb boneless chicken breasts

14fl. oz coconut milk

1 tablespoon dried chipotle flakes

2 small mangos

Preparation Method

1. Peel the mango and cut it in about 1 inch cubes.
2. Pour coconut milk in a slow cooker along with the mango cubes and mango's pit.
3. Cut the chicken in 1 inch cubes and put them in the cooker.
4. Stir in well the chipotle flakes.
5. Let it cook on low heat for 6 hours.

The delicious slow cooker coconut chicken is ready to serve.

Crock Pot Jamaican Wings

Serving Size

4 – 5 servings

Nutritional Facts (Values per Serving)

Calories/serving: 70

Total Carbohydrate: 3 g

Sodium: 128 mg

Protein: 5 g

Cholesterol: 19 mg

Total Fat: 4 g

Ingredients

4 lbs chicken wings

1 tablespoon coconut oil

1 tablespoon apple cider vinegar

2 tablespoon Jamaican Jerk seasoning

¼ cup fresh orange juice

1 lime

2 tablespoons coconut aminos

Preparation Method

1. Heat coconut oil in a skillet over medium-high heat.
2. Stir chicken in it for about 5 minutes or till it becomes light brown.
3. Now coat the chicken wings with the Jamaican jerk seasoning.
4. In another bowl, mix well the orange juice, apple cider vinegar and coconut aminos. Squeeze the lime in it and stir well.
5. Put the coated chicken in a plastic bag and pour the juice mixture on top of it.

6. Make sure all the wings are coated with the juice marinade.

7. Let it sit in the fridge overnight.

8. Pour the chicken and if there is any sauce in the plastic bag, in a slow cooker.

9. Let it cook on low heat for 4 hours.

The appetizing Crock Pot Jamaican Wings are ready to serve.

Slow Cooker BBQ Chicken

Serving Size

Serves 4

Nutritional Facts (Values per Serving)

Calories/serving: 162

Total Carbohydrate: 9 g

Sodium: 380 mg

Protein: 16.3 g

Cholesterol: 45 mg

Total Fat: 6.2 g

Ingredients

1 whole chicken,

2 teaspoon paprika

1 medium sized white onion (sliced)

1 teaspoon onion powder

1 teaspoon cayenne

1 teaspoon dried thyme

Half teaspoon garlic powder

1 teaspoon sea salt

1 teaspoon white pepper

Half teaspoon black pepper

Preparation Method

1. Remove and giblets of the chicken and wash it.
2. Dry the chicken thoroughly using a paper towel.
3. Take a slow cooker and line it with sliced onions.

4. Now place the whole chicken in the cooker on top of the onions.

5. In another bowl, add all the remaining ingredients and spices and mix them well.

6. Now coat this mixture over the entire chicken. Use your hands to do this and make sure every part of the chicken, inside and out is coated with it.

7. Cover the cooker and let it cook on low heat for 6 hours.

The delicious Slow Cooker BBQ Chicken is ready to serve.

Paleo Crock Pot Pulled Chicken with Spicy Sauce

Serving Size

2 – 3 servings

Nutritional Facts (Values per Serving)

Calories/serving: 343

Total Carbohydrate: 8.8 g

Sodium: 1225 mg

Protein: 38.9 g

Cholesterol: 112 mg

Total Fat: 16.7 g

Ingredients

3 lbs chicken breasts (boneless and skinless)

12 garlic cloves

2 lbs red bell peppers (seeded)

1 medium sized white onion (finely chopped)

1 cup tomato sauce

Half teaspoon thyme

Half teaspoon oregano

1 cup distilled water

Half teaspoon basil

Preparation Method

1. Roast the seeded bell peppers with half of the garlic cloves.
2. Puncture the chicken breasts with the tip of a sharp knife.
3. Stuff the remaining garlic cloves in the chicken.
4. Take a crock pot and add chopped onion, water and tomato sauce in it. Mix well.

5. Now add basil, oregano and thyme in the cooker. Stir all the ingredients well.

6. Put the chicken breasts in the crock pot. Make sure the chicken is at least halfway immersed in the liquid in the pot.

7. Add the roasted red peppers and garlic in the pot. Spread them to coat the entire chicken.

8. Let on cook on low heat for 5 hours.

9. Carefully take out the chicken in a bowl and shred it with the help of two forks.

10. Take out the remaining sauce from the crock pot and put in the blender.

11. Blend it for just a few seconds. Do not blend it finely. The final blended sauce should be slightly chunky.

12. Remove your chicken breasts from your slow cooker, transfer them to a large bowl and shred them with 2 forks.

13. Pour the sauce over the shredded chicken.

You can serve it as it is or can mix the sauce in the chicken.

Crock Pot Indian Chicken Curry

Serving Size

4 – 5 servings

Nutritional Facts (Values per Serving)

Calories/serving: 432

Total Carbohydrate: 20 g

Sodium: 411 mg

Protein: 46 g

Cholesterol: 188 mg

Total Fat: 17.9 g

Ingredients

3 lbs boneless chicken cubes

1 tablespoon coconut oil

1 teaspoon cumin seeds

1 teaspoon mustard seeds

¼ teaspoon fenugreek seeds

1 teaspoon red pepper flakes

Half teaspoon fennel seeds

1 cup crushed tomatoes

2 medium sized onions (sliced)

Half cup coconut cream

Half cup chicken stock

Cilantro to garnish

Marinade Ingredients

6 garlic cloves (minced)

Half small sized ginger (crushed)

1 teaspoon turmeric powder

1 tablespoon ground coriander

8 curry leaves

1 teaspoon chili powder

2 cinnamon sticks

1 lemongrass stalk (chop the white parts of the stalk)

2 teaspoon salt

6 cardamom pods

Lemon juice of 1 fresh lemon

1 tablespoon black pepper

¼ cup apple cider vinegar

1 cup coconut milk

2 bay leaves

5 dried chilies (whole)

Preparation Method

1. Roast cumin seeds, mustard seeds, fenugreek seeds, red pepper flakes and fennel seeds in a shallow pan over medium heat for 5 minutes.

2. Then put all these spice in a grinder/food processor and grind them thoroughly.

3. Take it out in a large bowl and add lemon juice, ginger, garlic, turmeric powder, salt and black pepper in it.

4. Mix all the ingredients well.

5. Now mix in it all the marinade ingredients.

6. Put chicken in this bowl and mix it well. Make sure all the chicken cubes are coated with the marinade.

7. Let it marinade for 4 - 5 hours.

8. Heat coconut oil in a pan on low heat.//
9. Fry onions in it till they become soft and light golden.
10. Put the fried onions and marinated chicken in a slow cooker.
11. Top it up with the tomato paste and chicken stock. Mix all the ingredients well.
12. Cover the cooker and let it cook on low heat for 6 hours.
13. Mix coconut cream in it and stir for a few minutes.
14. Cook it for another 15 minutes on high heat.

Serve hot with cooked rice.

Crock Pot Thai Noodles

Serving Size

4 – 5 servings

Nutritional Facts (Values per Serving)

Calories/serving: 310

Total Carbohydrate: 53.1 g

Sodium: 352 mg

Protein: 12.4 g

Cholesterol: 10.9 mg

Total Fat: 6.1 g

Ingredients

3 lbs skinless chicken breasts (cut into strips)

1 cup chicken stock

2 medium sized green onions (chopped)

Half of bean sprouts

1 large carrot (shredded)

1 tablespoon of Coconut Aminos (substitute: replace soy sauce)

2 medium sized zucchinis (sliced in the form of noodles)

2 teaspoons ginger powder

1 cup coconut milk

1 teaspoon cayenne pepper

2 tablespoons of sunflower butter

2 teaspoons paleo fish sauce

1 teaspoon crushed red pepper

2 garlic cloves (minced)

Salt and Pepper to taste

Preparation Method

1. Season the chicken strips with half of the cayenne pepper, half of the ginger powder, salt and pepper.

2. Add coconut milk and chicken stock in a slow cooker. Mix well.

3. Add in it, sunflower butter, fish sauce, coconut aminos, minced garlic, chopped onions, red pepper and the remaining ginger powder and cayenne pepper.

4. Stir till the butter completely dissolves.

5. Put the seasoned chicken strips on top of it.

6. In another bowl, mix the zucchini noodles, shredded carrot and bean sprouts.

7. Light put the vegetable noodles on the top of chicken in the cooker.

8. Let it cook on low heat for 5 hours.

9. Once the chicken is fully cooked, take out the noodles first and drain if there any liquid in it.

10. Mix the chicken strips with the sauce in the cooker.

11. Set the noodles in the serving tray and pour the chicken mixture on top of it.

Serve it hot.

Crock Pot Chicken Cacciatora

Serving Size

Serves 2

Nutritional Facts (Values per Serving)

Calories/serving: 196

Total Carbohydrate: 4.8 g

Sodium: 110 mg

Protein: 37 g

Cholesterol: 92 mg

Total Fat: 2.2 g

Ingredients

1 lb boneless chicken cubes

3 large bell peppers; green, red and yellow (seeded and sliced)

3 tablespoons olive oil

1 whole garlic clove

2 garlic cloves (minced)

1 medium sized white onion (sliced)

1 large celery stalk (finely chopped)

1 cup chopped tomatoes

Salt to taste

Preparation Method

1. Except for the chopped tomatoes, put all the ingredients in a slow cooker. Mix well.

2. Now put the tomatoes on top of the ingredients in cooker.

3. Cover and let it cook on low heat for 8 hours.

The appetizing crock pot chicken cacciatora is ready to serve.

Slow Cooker Spicy Cilantro Wings

Serving Size

4 – 5 servings

Nutritional Facts (Values per Serving)

Calories/serving: 301

Total Carbohydrate: 9.1 g

Sodium: 829.7 mg

Protein: 55.7 g

Cholesterol: 136.9 mg

Total Fat: 3.2 g

Ingredients

4 lbs chicken wings

2 teaspoons olive oil

Half cup lemon juice

1 garlic clove (minced)

Half cup fresh cilantro

1 teaspoon red chili powder

1 teaspoon cayenne pepper

1 teaspoon ground cumin

1 teaspoon black pepper

1 teaspoon sea salt

Preparation Method

1. Slightly brown the chicken pieces in pan.

2. Sprinkle red chili powder, cayenne pepper, ground cumin, black pepper and sea salt. Mix well so that all the wings get all the spices.

3. To make the marinade, put the cilantro, olive oil, lemon juice and minced garlic in a food processor.

4. Blend till it become a consistent paste.

5. Put the chicken in plastic bag and pour the marinade in it.

6. Let it sit the fridge for a couple of hours.

7. Pour out all the contents of the plastic bag in the crock pot and let it cook on low heat for 4 hours. If you are in a hurry, cook it on high heat for 2 hours.

Serve with tomato ketchup.

Smoked Crock Pot Meatloaf

Serving Size

4 – 5 servings

Nutritional Facts (Values per Serving)

Calories/serving: 243

Total Carbohydrate: 10.9 g

Sodium: 658 mg

Protein: 29 g

Cholesterol: 122 mg

Total Fat: 8.5 g

Ingredients

2 lbs lean ground chicken

4 ounces bacon (cooked and chopped)

2 medium sized green onions (diced)

1 small white onion (chopped)

2 eggs (whisked)

2 stalks celery (finely chopped)

1 teaspoon thyme

2 teaspoons dried oregano

2 teaspoons smoked paprika

1 teaspoon black pepper

2 teaspoons garlic powder

Ingredients for the Sauce

¼ cup tomato sauce

2 teaspoons smoked paprika

3 tablespoon Dijon mustard

1 teaspoon apple cider vinegar

2 teaspoons garlic powder

Preparation Method

1. Mix all the sauce ingredients in a bowl to make the loaf sauce. Set it aside.

2. In another large bowl, mix the ground meat, whisked eggs, chopped bacon, green onions, white onion, celery, thyme, oregano, smoked paprika, black pepper and garlic powder.

3. Mix thoroughly all the ingredients and form of loaf of it.

4. Put the meatloaf in a crock pot and press it a little. Make sure you keep the loaf an inch away from the sides of the pot.

5. Pour the loaf sauce on top of the loaf.

6. Cover the pot and let it cook on low heat for 5 – 6 hours.

Once cooked, take it out, slice and serve.

Paleo Slow Cooker Beef Recipes

Paleo Beef Tacos

Serving Size

4 – 5 servings

Nutritional Facts (Values per Serving)

Calories/serving: 211

Total Carbohydrate: 17 g

Sodium: 277 mg

Protein: 11 g

Cholesterol: 28 mg

Total Fat: 11.3 g

Ingredients

3 lbs chuck roast

½ ounce taco seasoning

16 ounce salsa

8 ounce taco sauce

1 cup water

Preparation Method

1. Put the chuck roast on large piece of plastic wrap.
2. Pour the taco seasoning over it and use your hand to spread it over the entire roast. Make sure the roast is thoroughly coated with the seasoning.
3. Wrap the roast the in the plastic.
4. Then wrap it in a piece of aluminum foil.
5. Put it in the refrigerator to marinate for at least 2 hours.
6. Then unwrap the roast and put it in a slow cooker.

7. Add salsa and water in it.
8. Let it cook on low heat for 8 to 9 hours.
9. Carefully take it out and shred the meat with 2 two forks.
10. Discard if there is any liquid remaining in the cooker.
11. Put the shredded meat back in the cooker.
12. Add the taco sauce and stir it.
13. Cover the pot and let it cook on high heat for another 15 minutes.

Enjoy the delectable paleo beef tacos.

Paleo Beef and Mushroom Meatloaf

Serving Size

2 – 3 servings

Nutritional Facts (Values per Serving)

Calories/serving: 470

Total Carbohydrate: 14 g

Sodium: 850 mg

Protein: 36.2 g

Cholesterol: 170 mg

Total Fat: 29 g

Ingredients

½ lbs grass fed ground beef

3 cups button mushrooms (sliced)

1 egg

3 ounces goat cheese

2 tablespoons granulated garlic

2 tablespoons oregano

2 tablespoons parsley

1 tablespoon dried rosemary

Half teaspoon sea salt

Half teaspoon black pepper

Preparation Method

1. Mix the grounded beef with egg and all the ingredients except mushrooms and goat cheese.

2. After mixing it thoroughly, press it down in the bowl to flatten it as much as possible.

3. Put the cheese in the center of the flattened beef mixture and wrap the beef around it.

4. Make sure the entire log of cheese is encased in the beef.

5. Press the mushroom slices in the meatloaf and put it in the slow cooker.

6. Let it cook on low heat for 6 hours.

Serve it hot.

Slow Cooker Sweet Potato Casserole

Serving Size

2 – 3 servings

Nutritional Facts (Values per Serving)

Calories/serving: 330

Total Carbohydrate: 11 g

Sodium: 190 mg

Protein: 23 g

Cholesterol: 210 mg

Total Fat: 21.2 g

Ingredients

2 lbs lean ground beef

½ lb bacon (diced)

3 large sweet potatoes

8 eggs (whisked)

1 large sized white onion (chopped)

1 large sized red onion (chopped)

Coconut oil to grease

Spices

1 teaspoon paprika

1 teaspoon Cayenne pepper

1 teaspoon garlic powder

1 teaspoon black pepper

1 teaspoon dried oregano

Preparation Method

1. Brown the diced bacon in a pan and set it aside.
2. Peel the sweet potatoes and microwave them for 3 minutes. Now slice them thinly.
3. Put the chopped onions and ground beef in a deep skillet.
4. Season it will all the spices.
5. Cook till the onion becomes translucent.
6. Now grease a crock pot with a bit of coconut oil.
7. Line the bottom of the pot with half of the sliced sweet potatoes.
8. Next, set a layer of half of the cooked beef, followed by a layer of half of the cooked bacon.
9. Repeat the layering with the remaining ingredients.
10. Top it up with beaten eggs.
11. Cover the pot and let it cook on low heat for 6 hours.
12. Once it is cooked, let it cool completely.

Slice and serve.

Slow Cooker Beefy Stew

Serving Size

3 – 4 servings

Nutritional Facts (Values per Serving)

Calories/serving: 321

Total Carbohydrate: 11.8 g

Sodium: 235 mg

Protein: 24.1 g

Cholesterol: 53.3 mg

Total Fat: 18.3 g

Ingredients

2 lbs beef stew meat

1 sweet potato (sliced)

2 cups whole shiitake mushrooms

2 cups button mushrooms (sliced)

2 cups baby portobello mushrooms

1 cup white onion (sliced)

8 – 10 baby carrots

2 cups beef broth

4 garlic cloves (minced)

2 bay leaves

Half cup balsamic vinegar

1 tablespoon dried oregano

1 teaspoon dried sage

1 tablespoon dried rosemary

Sea salt to taste

Black pepper to taste

Preparation Method

1. Put all the three type of mushrooms along with the sliced onions in a slow cooker.
2. Put meat on top of it.
3. Top it up with baby carrots and sweet potatoes.
4. Add the remaining ingredients and let it cook on low heat for 7 – 8 hours.

Serve it hot.

Slow Cooker Tongue with Red Sauce

Serving Size

Serves 2

Nutritional Facts (Values per Serving)

Calories/serving: 346

Total Carbohydrate: 13.6 g

Sodium: 278.2 mg

Protein: 22 g

Cholesterol: 119 mg

Total Fat: 22 g

Ingredients

1 beef tongue

3 bay leaves

1 onion (sliced)

3 garlic cloves (minced)

Sea salt to taste

Black pepper to taste

Distilled water

Ingredients for the Sauce

1 red bell pepper (roasted, peeled and diced)

2 large tomatoes (sliced)

1 onion (diced)

3 garlic cloves (minced)

1 Serrano pepper (roasted and diced)

6 oz. tomato paste

1 teaspoon oregano

1 teaspoon thyme

Sea salt to taste

Black pepper to taste

Preparation Method

1. Sauté 1 diced onion, 3 minced garlic, Serrano pepper and red pepper in a pan over medium heat.
2. When the onions become translucent, add in the remaining sauce ingredients and stir well.
3. Let it simmer on low heat for 30 minutes.
4. While the sauce is on heat, let's work on the beef tongue.
5. Wash the beef tongue thoroughly under cold water and dry it with a paper towel.
6. Line the bottom of the slow cooker with the remaining sliced onion, bay leaves and crushed garlic.
7. Put the tongue on top of it.
8. Sprinkle sea salt and black pepper on the tongue.
9. Add enough water in the cooker to immerse the tongue completely.
10. Cover the slow cooker and let it cook on low heat for 8 hours.
11. Carefully take the tongue out of the cooker and peel it skin.
12. Shred it using 2 forks.

Spread the sauce over the shredded tongue and enjoy.

Paleo Rib Beef N Bacon Burgers

Serving Size

6 – 7 servings

Nutritional Facts (Values per Serving)

Calories/serving: 513

Total Carbohydrate: 25 g

Sodium: 1301 mg

Protein: 46.3 g

Cholesterol: 110 mg

Total Fat: 24 g

Ingredients

4 lbs Beef Short Ribs

1 ½ lbs

7 - 8 medium sized pieces of bacon

Half cup beef broth (substitute: chicken broth or vegetable broth)

1 ½ cups Paleo Maple Mustard Sauce (some extra sauce for topping)

4 garlic cloves (crushed)

1 small yellow onion (finely chopped)

Sea salt to taste

Black pepper to taste

Preparation Method

1. Put the short ribs and broth in a slow cooker.
2. Add the paleo maple mustard sauce, half of the minced garlic cloves, salt and black pepper in it.
3. Cover the cooker and let it cook on low heat for 8 - 10 hours.

4. While the ribs are cooking, preheat the oven to 405 degrees.

5. Place the bacon pieces in a baking sheet and put it in the preheated oven for 12 – 15 minutes.

6. When the bacon is cooked, take it out set aside.

7. When the ribs are fully cooked, take it out in a bowl and shred it.

8. Add the grass fed ground beef, remaining minced garlic cloves, chopped yellow onion, salt and black pepper in the rib containing bowl. Mix all the ingredients thoroughly.

9. Form the burger sized patties with this mixture.

10. Heat a large skillet over medium heat.

11. Once the skillet is hot, fry the patties in it.

Layer the burger in the following sequence.

Burger patty - bacon – mustard sauce and Enjoy!

Paleo Slow Cooker Pork Recipes

Crock Pot Pork Waffle Bars

Serving Size

4 – 6 servings

Nutritional Facts (Values per Serving)

Calories/serving: 750

Total Carbohydrate: 6.2 g

Sodium: 1608 mg

Protein: 138 g

Cholesterol: 236 mg

Total Fat: 43 g

Ingredients

2 lbs pork butt

3 teaspoons garlic powder

1 medium sized yellow onion (sliced)

1 teaspoon onion powder

Sea salt to taste

Black Pepper to taste

5 – 6 layers of cooked bacon for topping

Ingredients for the Waffles

2 cups almond flour

3 eggs

Half teaspoon garlic powder

Half cup coconut milk

3 medium sized pieces of bacon (cooked and chopped)

Half teaspoon baking soda

2 tablespoons chives (chopped)

2 tablespoons bacon fat

Sea salt to taste

Black Pepper to taste

Ingredients for the Mayo Sauce

⅔ cup avocado oil

1 teaspoon lemon juice

¼ teaspoon garlic powder

1 egg

1 teaspoon Dijon mustard

1 teaspoon maple syrup

Sea salt to taste

Black Pepper to taste

Preparation Method

1. Add the pork butt in the slow cooker with sliced onion, salt, garlic powder, black pepper and onion powder.

2. Cover it and let it cook on low heat for 7 - 8 hours.

3. Once it is completely cooked, turn of the heat and shred the pork in cooker using 2 forks. Set it aside.

4. While the pork is cooking, let's make the mayo sauce. Put all the ingredients of the mayo sauce except for the maple syrup in a blender.

5. Turn on the blender and wait till the mixture become thick.

6. When the mixture is thick enough, add maple syrup it and mix it thoroughly with a spoon.

7. Take it out in a container and out it the refrigerator to cool.

8. To make the waffles, preheat the waffle iron on medium heat.

9. Mix the almond flour, garlic powder, baking soda and a pinch of salt and black pepper.

10. Whisk the eggs in a separate bowl and then add them in the flour mixture.

11. Then add in it the bacon fat, coconut milk, chopped bacon and chives. Mix all the ingredients well.

12. Pour this batter in the waffle iron. Two tablespoons would make 1 small waffle.

13. Cook until it is crispy.

14. Layer the waffle in the following sequence.

Waffle - Mayo Sauce - Shredded Pork - Slice of bacon - Mayo sauce – Waffle.

Caramelized Pork Treat

Serving Size

4 – 6 servings

Nutritional Facts (Values per Serving)

Calories/serving: 390

Total Carbohydrate: 61.8 g

Sodium: 67.2 mg

Protein: 26.3 g

Cholesterol: 74 mg

Total Fat: 6.2 g

Ingredients

2 lbs pork loin

4 brown plantains (peeled and sliced in half)

3 cups beef broth

1 medium sized yellow onion (sliced)

4 tablespoons coconut milk

2 tablespoons coconut oil

1 tablespoon garlic powder

1 teaspoon onion powder

1 teaspoon cinnamon powder

Sea salt to taste

Black Pepper to taste

Preparation Method

1. In a crock pot, add the pork loin, sliced yellow onion, beef broth garlic powder, onion powder, salt and pepper.

2. Cover and let it cook for 9 – 10 hours.

3. When the pork is fully cooked, shred it using two forks and set it aside.

4. Heat the coconut oil in pan over medium heat.

5. When the oil is hot, put the sliced plantains in it.

6. Add the cinnamon powder and salt in it.

7. Cook on both sides till the plantains become soft.

8. Now put the cooked plantains in a food processor and blend it for a few minutes.

9. While the blender is still on, add the coconut milk and blend till you it becomes a smooth plantain puree.

To serve, put a blob of plantain puree on the plate. Top it up with some shredded pork.

Paleo Sausage Pie

Serving Size

4 – 6 servings

Nutritional Facts (Values per Serving)

Calories/serving: 654

Total Carbohydrate: 47.8 g

Sodium: 1497 mg

Protein: 30.5 g

Cholesterol: 343.2 mg

Total Fat: 37.5 g

Ingredients

1 lb pork sausage

1 sweet potato

8 eggs

1 yellow onion (chopped)

2 teaspoons dried basil

1 tablespoon garlic powder

Coconut oil to grease the pot

Salt to taste

Black Pepper to taste

Preparation Method

1. Grease a crock pot with a little bit of coconut oil.

2. Add in it the shredded sweet potato, chopped onion, basil, garlic powder, salt and pepper. Mix well.

3. Whisk the eggs and put them in the crock pot.

4. Mix all the ingredients, cover the pot and let it cook on low for 7 – 8 hours. Slice it and serve with tomato ketchup.

Apple and Ginger Pork

Serving Size

6 – 8 servings

Nutritional Facts (Values per Serving)

Calories/serving: 298

Total Carbohydrate: 15.2 g

Sodium: 541 mg

Protein: 25.6 g

Cholesterol: 87 mg

Total Fat: 14.7 g

Ingredients

2 lbs pork roast

2/3 chicken broth

2 medium sized apples (cored and sliced)

1 medium sized yellow onion (sliced)

1 bay leaf

2 tablespoons grated ginger

1 tablespoon raw honey

2 garlic cloves (peeled and minced)

1 teaspoon cinnamon powder

Half teaspoon smoked paprika

1 teaspoon salt

Half teaspoon black pepper

Preparation Method

1. In a crock pot, add chicken broth, sliced onions, pork and sliced apples. Mix well.

2. Now add all the remaining ingredients and stir.

3. Cover the pot and cook on low heat for 9 – 10 hours, then on high heat for 7 – 8 hours.

4. Once the pork is cooked, use two forks to shred the meat.

Serve it with mayo dip and tomato ketchup.

Green Slow Cooker Pork

Serving Size

6 – 8 servings

Nutritional Facts (Values per Serving)

Calories/serving: 309

Total Carbohydrate: 40.6 g

Sodium: 272.7 mg

Protein: 29.3 g

Cholesterol: 57 mg

Total Fat: 29 g

Ingredients

2 lbs pork roast

2 cups chicken broth

1 medium sized yellow onion (diced)

8 oz. canned tomatoes (diced)

4 oz. canned green chilies (diced)

2 garlic cloves (crushed)

2 anaheim pepper (seeds removed and diced)

1 poblano chili (seeds removed and diced)

1-2 jalapeno peppers (chopped)

1 teaspoon oregano

Half teaspoon paprika

Half teaspoon cumin

1 teaspoon white pepper

Half teaspoon cayenne pepper

Half teaspoon sage

1 teaspoon salt

Preparation Method

1. Put the pork roast in a slow cooker along with the tomatoes and green chilies.
2. Put all the remaining ingredients in it. Mix well.
3. Finally, add the broth in the cooker.
4. Cover it and let it cook on low heat for 7 – 8 hours.
5. Once the pork is fully cooked, shred it using two forks.
6. Mix it well with all the ingredients in the pot and serve it hot.

Paleo Pork and Butternut Stew

Serving Size

4 – 5 servings

Nutritional Facts (Values per Serving)

Calories/serving: 431

Total Carbohydrate: 20.8 g

Sodium: 270 mg

Protein: 52.5 g

Cholesterol: 135 mg

Total Fat: 14.9 g

Ingredients

2 ½ lbs pork loin (cut in 1 inch cubes)

1 cup chicken broth

2 shallots (peeled and chopped)

4 cups butternut squash

9 garlic cloves (minced)

¼ cup coconut milk

2 leeks (trimmed and diced)

4 celery stalks (diced)

2 teaspoons allspice

2 teaspoons lemon juice

2 teaspoons sea salt

Preparation Method

1. Put the pork cubes and all the vegetables in a crock pot. Mix well.
2. Add the remaining ingredients and spices in it. Stir well.

3. Cover the pot and let it cook on low heat for 7 - 8 hours.

Serve it hot!

Crock Pot Pork Honey Ribs

Serving Size

2 – 3 servings

Nutritional Facts (Values per Serving)

Calories/serving: 189

Total Carbohydrate: 2.8 g

Sodium: 227 mg

Protein: 22.3 g

Cholesterol: 72.6 mg

Total Fat: 9.4 g

Ingredients

1 lb pork ribs

2 tablespoons of bacon fat

1 medium sized white onion (chopped)

4 garlic cloves (minced)

1 cup broth

2 oz. tomato paste

1 teaspoon mustard powder

1 tablespoon apple cider vinegar 1 tablespoon molasses

2 tablespoons red chili powder

1 teaspoon maple syrup (substitute: raw honey)

Preparation Method

1. To make the sauce, heat the bacon fat in pan over medium heat.

2. Add the chopped onion in it and cook till it becomes translucent.

3. Then add all the remaining ingredients. Mix well.

4. Reduce the heat to low and let it simmer for 10 -15 minutes.
5. Now put the pork ribs in the slow cooker.
6. Pour the sauce over the ribs.
7. Cover and let it cook on low heat for 7 – 8 hours.

The scrumptious crock pot pork honey ribs are ready to serve.

Paleo Slow Cooker Mix Meat Treats

Paleo Crock Pot Supreme Pizza

Serving Size

3 – 4 servings

Nutritional Facts (Values per Serving)

Calories/serving: 406

Total Carbohydrate: 17g

Sodium: 925 mg

Protein: 43 g

Cholesterol: 110 mg

Total Fat: 19.5 g

Ingredients

1 lb boneless chicken breast (thinly sliced)

Half pound pepperoni (thinly sliced)

1 medium sized eggplant (thinly sliced)

3 garlic cloves (crushed)

3 cups tomato sauce

1 tablespoon olive oil

1 cup black olives (sliced)

1 tablespoon Italian seasoning

1 cup Mozzarella cheese (grated)

Half cup Parmesan cheese (grated)

Sea salt to taste

Parsley to garnish

Preparation Method

1. Soak the eggplant slices in large bowl of water.
2. Allow it to soak for an hour.
3. Drain it, sprinkle some salt on it and put it between paper towels. Let it be this way for 30 minutes.
4. In the meanwhile, mix olive oil and tomato sauce in a bowl.
5. Pound the chicken slices with a meat mallet. Make them as thin as possible.
6. Set the ingredients in the cooker in the following sequence. Use half of the ingredients to make the first layer and remaining half for the second one.
7. Olive tomato sauce – dried eggplant slice - parmesan cheese – chicken - Olive tomato sauce - mozzarella cheese - black olive slices – pepperoni.
8. Repeat the sequence again to make the second layer.
9. Now let it cook on low heat for 5 hours.
10. Cook on high for 3 hours or low for 5 hours.
11. Slice it in the cooker if you cannot take it out all together in one piece.

Garnish with parsley and serve with tomato ketchup.

Crock Pot Pine Nut Meatballs

Serving Size

3 – 4 servings

Nutritional Facts (Values per Serving)

Calories/serving: 261

Total Carbohydrate: 6 g

Sodium: 98 mg

Protein: 28 g

Cholesterol: 122 mg

Total Fat: 14 g

Ingredients

2 lbs ground meat (It can be beef, turkey or lamb)

1 cup pine nuts

2 cups crushed tomatoes

4 eggs (whisked)

3 cups assorted veggies (grated)

3 cups fresh spinach

Salt to taste

Preparation Method

1. In a large bowl, mix the assorted grated vegetable, salt and whisked eggs well. Make sure every vegetable is coated with egg.

2. Add in the ground meat. Use your hand to thoroughly mix the meat in the egg coated vegetables.

3. Roll the meatballs in a golf ball size.

4. Line the bottom of a crock pot with crush tomatoes. (Don't use all. Just use enough tomatoes to cover the base of the pot)

5. Now cover the tomatoes with half of the spinach.

6. Next, put the meatballs in the pot.

7. Fill the gaps between the meatballs with the remaining crushed tomatoes.

8. Cover the meatballs with the remaining spinach and pine nuts.

9. Put the lid on the pot and let it cook on low heat for 5 – 6 hours.

The delicious crock pot pine nut meatballs are ready to serve.

Paleo Mexican Rice

Serving Size

1 – 2 servings

Nutritional Facts (Values per Serving)

Calories/serving: 60

Total Carbohydrate: 5.2 g

Sodium: 580 mg

Protein: 2.4 g

Cholesterol: 10 mg

Total Fat: 3.7 g

Ingredients

Half cup chicken stock (Substitute: Beef Stock)

1 large cauliflower

1 tablespoon tomatoes paste

2 yellow bell peppers (chopped)

3 medium sized tomatoes (chopped)

2 jalapeno peppers (seeded and diced)

1 medium sized white onion (chopped)

2 teaspoons ground cumin

1 teaspoon black pepper

1 tablespoon garlic powder

2 teaspoons cayenne pepper

1 teaspoon dried oregano

Salt to taste

Preparation Method

1. Remove the stems of the cauliflower and cut it in medium sized florets.
2. Mix tomato paste, chopped tomatoes and chicken stock in a crock pot.
3. Add all the remaining ingredients in the crock pot except for the cauliflower florets. Mix all the ingredients thoroughly.
4. Now add the florets in the pot. Stir well so that all the florets get properly coated in the ingredients.
5. Cover the pot and let it cook on low heat for 5 hours.
6. Once cooked, use a wooden spoon to slightly mash the florets.

Take it out and serve.

Slow Cooker Meaty Stuff

Serving Size

1 – 2 servings

Nutritional Facts (Values per Serving)

Calories/serving: 422

Total Carbohydrate: 13.6 g

Sodium: 305 mg

Protein: 57.9 g

Cholesterol: 168.7 mg

Total Fat: 11.8 g

Ingredients

6 ounces salt pork (cut in 1 inch cubes)

8 ounces boneless chicken (chopped)

Half cup apple cider vinegar

1 medium sized white onion (diced)

7 oz. tomato paste

1 cup water

2 tablespoons Dijon mustard

2 teaspoons dehydrated onion.

¼ cup raw honey

1 teaspoon garlic powder

1 teaspoon chili powder

1 tablespoon Spanish paprika

Preparation Method

1. In a skillet, brown the pork cubes and chopped chicken.

2. Add the diced onion and in it and stir.

3. Then add all the remaining ingredients in the skillet except for the tomato paste and water. Mix well.

4. Cook on medium-high heat till the pork and onions become light brown.

5. Now add the tomato paste and water. Mix well.

6. Pour the contents of the skillet in a crock pot.

7. Let it cook on low heat for 5 hours or on high heat for 2- 3 hours.

Enjoy!

Slow Cooker Meat Lovers

Serving Size

2 – 3 servings

Nutritional Facts (Values per Serving)

Calories/serving: 1036

Total Carbohydrate: 44 g

Sodium: 1274 mg

Protein: 61 g

Cholesterol: 200 mg

Total Fat: 68.6 g

Ingredients

1 lb pork (Substitute: turkey or chicken)

1 lb ground grass fed beef

Half lb bacon

1 large white onion (diced)

1 large red onion (diced)

2 habanero peppers

2 garlic cloves (minced)

3 bell peppers (colors of your choice)

2 cups crushed tomatoes

1 tablespoon cayenne pepper

1 teaspoon black pepper

1 teaspoon sea salt

Preparation Method

1. Brown the bacon in skillet and set it aside.

2. Brown the beef and pork in a bacon grease skillet. Sprinkle all the dried peppers and salt in it.

3. Put all the meat and bacon in a crock pot.

4. Cut the bell peppers and habanero in 1 inch cubes and add them in the crock pot.

5. Now add all the remaining ingredients in it. Mix well.

6. Let it cook on low heat for 6 hours.

7. Once it is completely cooked, pour it out in food processor and blend to make a thick paste.

Serve it with fresh bread.

Smokey Crock Pot Pulled Pork

Serving Size

8 – 10 servings

Nutritional Facts (Values per Serving)

Calories/serving: 560

Total Carbohydrate: 4.8 g

Sodium: 130 mg

Protein: 54 g

Cholesterol: 151 mg

Total Fat: 35.2 g

Ingredients

6 lbs pork shoulder

6 cloves garlic (peeled in cut in half)

2 small sized yellow onions (sliced)

Spices

2 tablespoon dehydrated onion (crushed)

¼ cup smoked paprika

1 tablespoon ground cumin

1 tablespoon black pepper

1 tablespoon chili powder

Preparation Method

1. Use the tip of knife to poke holes in the pork shoulder.
2. Press a garlic slice in every hole.
3. Mix all the spices in a large bowl.
4. Coat the garlic stuffed pork shoulder with spice mixture.

5. Line a crock pot with onion slices.

6. Put the pork shoulder on top of the onion.

7. Cover and let it cook for 9 -10 hours.

8. When the pork is fully cooked, use two forks shred the meat.

Serve it with fresh bread.

Slow Cooker Chicken and Eggplant Lasagna

Serving Size

2 – 3 servings

Nutritional Facts (Values per Serving)

Calories/serving: 165

Total Carbohydrate: 7.0 g

Sodium: 1461 mg

Protein: 26 g

Cholesterol: 79 mg

Total Fat: 3.3 g

Ingredients

1 large sized eggplant (sliced)

2 lbs chicken breasts, boneless (cut into chunks)

3 cups baby spinach

1 medium sized white onion (thinly sliced)

4 garlic cloves (crushed)

1 cup crumbled blue cheese

1 cup Hot Sauce

2 teaspoons fresh parsley

Salt to taste

Black pepper to taste

Preparation Method

1. Soak the eggplant slices in a large bowl water.
2. Let it sit for 30 minutes. Strain and dry them with paper towels.
3. Pound the chicken chunks with a meat mallet.

4. Sprinkle parsley, salt and pepper in the chicken. Mix well.

5. In another bowl, add crush garlic, hot sauce and sliced onion. Mix well.

6. Now layer the ingredients in a 6-quart crock pot in the following sequence. Use half of the ingredients to form the first layer and remaining half for the second layer.

7. Sauce mixture – eggplant slices – season chicken – spinach – cheese – Repeat.

8. Cover and let it cook on low heat for 5 hours or on high heat for 3 hours.

Slice and enjoy!

Slow Cooker Italian Treat

Serving Size

3 – 4 servings

Nutritional Facts (Values per Serving)

Calories/serving: 198

Total Carbohydrate: 1.2 g

Sodium: 214 mg

Protein: 32.2 g

Cholesterol: 87 mg

Total Fat: 5.9 g

Ingredients

3 lbs boneless beef (cut into big chunks)

½ crushed tomatoes

4 medium sized carrots (sliced)

2 cups chicken stock

1 white onion (sliced)

5 garlic cloves (minced)

1 tablespoon tomato paste

Spices

1 teaspoon garlic powder

1 teaspoon dried oregano

1 teaspoon dried basil

1 teaspoon sea salt

Half teaspoon thyme

Pinch of cinnamon powder

Pinch of crush red chili

Preparation Method

1. Add the beef chunks, sliced carrots, onion slices and garlic in a crock pot. Mix well.

2. Add all the spices and mix well.

3. Next, add the chicken stock, tomato paste and crushed tomatoes. Stir well to mix all the ingredients.

4. Cover the pot and let it cook on low heat for 5 - 6 hours.

The appetizing slow cooker Italian treat is ready to serve.

Paleo BBQ Flavored Coffee Roast

Serving Size

3 – 4 servings

Nutritional Facts (Values per Serving)

Calories/serving: 209

Total Carbohydrate: 6 g

Sodium: 244 mg

Protein: 28 g

Cholesterol: 82 mg

Total Fat: 7 g

Ingredients

2.5 lbs beef chuck roast

1 small red onion (sliced)

Half tablespoon coconut oil

¾ cup water

Seasonings

2 tablespoons coffee

1 tablespoon cumin

1 teaspoon unsweetened cocoa powder

Half teaspoon ground chipotle

¼ teaspoon cinnamon powder

1 tablespoon dried oregano

Half tablespoon garlic powder

1 teaspoon sea salt

Preparation Method

1. Mix all the seasonings in a bowl.//
2. Rub the seasonings mixture on the roast. Make sure every part of the roast is properly coated with it.
3. Heat coconut oil in a pan over medium - high heat.
4. Put the roast in it and stir for 4 minutes on each side.
5. Line the bottom of a slow cooker with slices of onion.
6. Put the roast on top of it.
7. Add water, cover the cooker and let it cook on low heat for 7 – 8 hours.

Serve it hot!

Slow Cooker Mexican Carnitas

Serving Size

4 – 5 servings

Nutritional Facts (Values per Serving)

Calories/serving: 258.2

Total Carbohydrate: 6 g

Sodium: 544.2 mg

Protein: 34 g

Cholesterol: 104 mg

Total Fat: 6.1 g

Ingredients

2.5 lbs pork butt (cut into small cubes)

Half cup barbecue sauce

1 teaspoon minced garlic

1 tablespoon raw honey

1 yellow onion (chopped)

2 medium sized tomatoes (diced)

1 tablespoon cumin

2 tablespoons orange juice

2 teaspoon onion powder

2 teaspoons lime juice

2 teaspoon chili powder

1 teaspoon garlic powder

¼ cup canned green chilies (diced)

Half teaspoon sea salt

Lettuce to serve

Preparation Method

1. Put all the ingredients in a slow cooker. Stir to mix.
2. Cover and let it coke on low heat for 7 – 8 hours.

Serve in lettuce wraps.

Slow Cooker Meatballs

Serving Size

2 – 3 servings

Nutritional Facts (Values per Serving)

Calories/serving: 179

Total Carbohydrate: 18 g

Sodium: 503.2 mg

Protein: 10.5 g

Cholesterol: 40 mg

Total Fat: 7.3 g

Ingredients for Meatballs

1 lb grass fed ground beef

2 eggs

1 lb pastured Italian sausage

¼ cup full fat coconut milk

2 cloves garlic (minced)

2 tablespoons fresh basil (chopped)

¼ cup parmesan cheese

2 tablespoons fresh oregano chopped)

¼ cup almond meal

1 tablespoon black pepper

1 tablespoon sea salt

Ingredients for Sauce

1 large can crushed tomatoes (approx. 28 oz.)

8 oz. tomato sauce

1 medium sized sweet onion (thinly sliced)

2 tablespoons fresh basil (chopped)

4 gloves garlic (minced)

2 tablespoons fresh thyme (chopped)

2 tablespoons fresh oregano (chopped)

1 tablespoon black pepper

1 tablespoon sea salt

Preparation Method

1. Toss all the ingredients for the meatballs in a large bowl.
2. Use your hand to mix well. Make sure all the ingredients are thoroughly mixed with the meat.
3. Make golf sized ball meatballs and set them aside.
4. To make the sauce, mix all sauce ingredients except for the sliced onion, in a large bowl.
5. Line the bottom of a crock pot with half of the onion slices.
6. Place half of the meatballs on top of the onions.
7. Top it up with half of the sauce.
8. Line the remaining onions.
9. Set the remaining meatballs and top it up with the remaining sauce.
10. Cover and let it cook on low heat for 8 hours. Enjoy!

Celebration Ribs

Serving Size

6 – 8 servings

Nutritional Facts (Values per Serving)

Calories/serving: 1497

Total Carbohydrate: 34.5 g

Sodium: 620.5 mg

Protein: 50 g

Cholesterol: 229 mg

Total Fat: 112.5 g

Ingredients

4 lbs beef short ribs

2 tablespoons bacon fat

3 celery stalks (washed and chopped)

750ml red wine

1 large onion (chopped)

3 cups beef stock

5 cloves garlic (minced)

3 medium sized carrots (peeled and chopped)

2 sweet potatoes (cut in large chunks)

8 oz. tomato paste

1 tablespoon oregano

1 tablespoon thyme

1 tablespoon rosemary

Pepper to taste

Salt to taste

Preparation Method

1. Set the oven to preheat at 350 degrees.
2. Season both side of the rib with salt and pepper.
3. Melt the bacon fat in an oven-safe crock pot and brown the ribs in it.
4. Remove the meat from the pot and sauté all the vegetables in it.
5. Add a little more salt and pepper.
6. Cook till the onion becomes translucent.
7. Then add the minced garlic and tomato paste.
8. Stir well then add the red wine and beef stock in it.
9. Add the back in the pot and let it boil for a minute.
10. Cover the pot and place it in the preheated oven for 2 hours.
11. After 2 hours, add sweet potatoes in it.
12. Cover and let it bake in the oven for another 30 minutes.
13. After 2 hours, add sweet potatoes in it.
14. Cover and let it bake in the oven for another 30 minutes.

Enjoy!

Slow Cooker Paleo Chicken Stuffed Peppers

Serving Size

    3 – 4 servings

Nutritional Facts (Values per Serving)

    Calories/serving: 379

    Total Carbohydrate: 22.2 g

    Sodium: 1190 mg

    Protein: 46 g

    Cholesterol: 126 mg

    Total Fat: 11.7 g

Ingredients

    4 whole chicken breasts

    ¼ cup canned chopped green peppers

    4 large bell peppers

    1 large tomato (diced)

    1 small onion (finely chopped)

    Half cup beef broth

    4 tablespoons taco seasoning

    2 cups salsa

    Shredded cheese to garnish

Preparation Method

1. Put the chicken breasts, chopped green peppers, diced tomato, chopped onion, beef broth, and taco seasoning in a slow cooker. Mix well.

2. Cover and let it cook on low heat for 7 – 8 hours.

3. When the chicken is fully cooked, let it cool for while.

4. Then shred the chicken by 2 forks and mix it well.

5. Cut the top of the bell peppers and take out all the seeds from it.

6. Wash it under cold water.

7. Stuff the chicken mixture in the peppers and line them in a baking tray.

8. Top it up with salsa and bake it at 350 degrees for 20 minutes.

Garnish with shredded cheese. Enjoy!

Paleo Italian Shrimp Marinara

Serving Size

Serves 2

Nutritional Facts (Values per Serving)

Calories/serving: 450

Total Carbohydrate: 17 g

Sodium: 1789 mg

Protein: 44.0 g

Cholesterol: 175 mg

Total Fat: 22 g

Ingredients

1 lb cooked shelled shrimp

16 oz canned diced tomatoes

6 oz. canned tomato paste

1 lb grated Parmesan cheese

2 tablespoons crushed parsley

1 lb spaghetti squash (cooked)

Half teaspoon dried basil

1 garlic clove (minced)

1 teaspoon dried oregano

1 teaspoon salt

¼ teaspoon pepper

Preparation Method

1. Add tomatoes, parsley, basil, salt, pepper, crushed garlic, tomato paste and oregano in a slow cooker. Mix well.

2. Cover and let it cook on low heat for 6 – 7 hours.

3. Now add the shrimps and stir.

4. Cover and let it cook on high heat for another 15 minutes.

5. Poke 10 holes in the spaghetti squash and microwave it for 8 minutes.

6. Let it cook for a while, then cut it in half and remove its seeds.

7. Set in on a serving tray and pour the shrimp gravy on top of it.

Top it up with parmesan cheese. Enjoy!

Meat 'n' Chili

Serving Size

3 – 4 servings

Nutritional Facts (Values per Serving)

Calories/serving: 355

Total Carbohydrate: 43 g

Sodium: 589 mg

Protein: 23.2 g

Cholesterol: 50 mg

Total Fat: 12 g

Ingredients

2 lbs grass fed ground beef

1 large yellow onion (chopped)

¼ cup 100% cacao powder (free from soy lecithin and added cacao butter)

4 stalks celery (diced)

1 bell pepper (chopped)

16 oz canned diced tomatoes

1 tablespoon bacon fat

6 oz. canned tomato paste

4 cloves garlic (crushed)

2 teaspoons ground cumin

1 teaspoon chili powder

1 teaspoon crushed red pepper

6 oz. Chipotle peppers in adobo sauce (optional)

1 teaspoon smoked paprika

1 teaspoon salt

1 teaspoon black pepper

Preparation Method

1. Melt and heat the bacon fat in a large skillet over medium heat.
2. Sauté the chopped onion and garlic in it.
3. Add beef in the pan and cook till it picks up brown color.
4. Now pour out the contents of the skillet in a crock pot.
5. Add all the remaining ingredients in the pot. Mix well.
6. Cover and let it cook on low heat for 7 – 8 hours. Enjoy!

Slow Cooker Jambalaya Stew

Serving Size

2 – 3 servings

Nutritional Facts (Values per Serving)

Calories/serving: 458

Total Carbohydrate: 38.2 g

Sodium: 1187 mg

Protein: 24.6 g

Cholesterol: 147 mg

Total Fat: 22.5 g

Ingredients

4 oz. chicken (cut in small cubes)

1 lb large shrimp, (raw and de-veined)

2 cups lady fingers

1 lb spicy Andouille sausage

5 cups chicken stock

1 large onion (diced)

3 tablespoons Cajun Seasoning

4 bell peppers, (chopped, any color of your choice)

1 head cauliflower

2 cloves garlic (minced)

25 oz. organic diced tomatoes

2 bay leaves

¼ cup hot sauce

Preparation Method

1. Add the chicken stock onions, lady fingers, chopped peppers, chicken, garlic, hot sauce, Cajun seasoning and bay leaves in a slow cooker. Mix well.

2. Cover and let it cook on low heat for 6 hours.

3. Uncover, add in the sausages and let it cook for another 10 minutes.

4. Meanwhile, put the cauliflower in a food processor and run till it takes the form of rice.

5. Add the cauliflower rice and shrimp in the pot and let it cook for another 30 minutes.

Serve and Enjoy!

Crockpot Sweet Butter

Serving Size

Makes 1 small jar

Nutritional Facts (Values per Serving)

Calories/serving: 31

Total Carbohydrate: 8 g

Sodium: 1 mg

Protein: 0.0 g

Cholesterol: 0.0 mg

Total Fat: 0.0 g

Ingredients

20 dried black figs

1 cup apple cider

6 red apples

Half cup honey (substitute: maple syrup)

Half teaspoon ground cloves

¼ teaspoon nutmeg

3 tablespoons ground cinnamon

¼ teaspoon salt

Preparation Method

1. Remove the stems of the figs and cut in half.
2. Peel, core and dice the apples.
3. Put all the ingredients in a crock pot. Mix well.
4. Cover and let it cook on low heat for 7 – 8 hours.
5. Pour out the contents of the pot in the food processor.

6. Blend till it become a smooth puree.

7. Store it in the fridge to cool.

Enjoy with bread!

Crock Pot Short Rib Tacos

Serving Size

3 – 4 servings

Nutritional Facts (Values per Serving)

Calories/serving: 843

Total Carbohydrate: 121.4 g

Sodium: 2147 mg

Protein: 12.6 g

Cholesterol: 41.5 mg

Total Fat: 28.9 g

Ingredients

2 lbs pork short ribs (boneless)

2 teaspoons garlic powder

2 tablespoons maple syrup

6 strips of bacon (cooked and chopped)

3 tablespoons hot sauce

8 ounce green chilies

2 large green onions (chopped)

Salt to taste

Ingredients for Tortillas

3 eggs (whisked)

2 tablespoons coconut flour

Half cup coconut milk

¼ teaspoon salt

Preparation Method

1. Add short ribs, maple syrup, garlic powder and salt in a crock pot.
2. Cover the pot and let it cook on low for 9 – 10- hours.
3. Once cooked, remove the ribs from the pot and shred them with two forks. Set it aside.
4. To make the tortillas, put all the tortilla ingredients in a large bowl. Whisk well.
5. Heat a non stick pan over medium heat.
6. Pour the tortilla mixture in the pan in the shape of pancakes.
7. Cook for about a minute on each side.
8. In a bowl, mix the green chilies and hot sauce. Microwave it for about 2 minutes and then chop the chilies.
9. Layer the tortilla in the following sequence.

Tortilla - Shredded pork – chopped green chilies – bacon - green onions. Repeat.

Enjoy!

Stuffed Peppers Delight

Serving Size

Makes 5 stuffed peppers

Nutritional Facts (Values per Serving)

Calories/serving: 443

Total Carbohydrate: 37.4 g

Sodium: 917.7 mg

Protein: 19.6 g

Cholesterol: 51.5 mg

Total Fat: 24.0 g

Ingredients

1 lb ground Italian hot sausage

Half head of cauliflower

5 bell peppers (different colors)

1 small white onion (chopped)

8 oz canned tomato paste

2 teaspoons dried thyme

2 teaspoons dried basil

8 cloves garlic (chopped)

2 teaspoons dried oregano

Preparation Method

1. Cut the top of the bell peppers and remove the seed out of them. (Save the tops for later use).

2. Chop the cauliflower in a food processor till it takes the shape of rice.

3. Add chopped garlic, onion, dried oregano, dried basil and dried thyme in the cauliflower rice. Mix well.

4. Then add the sausages and tomato paste in it. Mix well
5. Stuff this mixture in the bell peppers.
6. Line them in the slow cooker and put the pepper tops on them.
7. Cover and let it cook on low heat for 6 hours.

The delectable stuffed peppers delight is ready to serve.

Hawaiian Paleo Salad

Serving Size

4 – 6 servings

Nutritional Facts (Values per Serving)

Calories/serving: 370

Total Carbohydrate: 42 g

Sodium: 264 mg

Protein: 22.3 g

Cholesterol: 26 mg

Total Fat: 15 g

Ingredients

3 lbs pork shoulder

2 tablespoons bacon fat

Half cup chopped pepperoni

2 cups chopped pineapple

4 garlic cloves

1 medium sized yellow onion (sliced)

2 hearts of romaine lettuce (chopped)

4 oz. button mushrooms (sliced)

1 red bell pepper (seeds removed and chopped)

1 teaspoon garlic powder

Salt to taste

Preparation Method

1. Use the tip of sharp knife to poke 4 holes in the pork shoulder.
2. Peel and stuff a clove of garlic in each hole.

3. Line the bottom of a slow cooker with sliced onions.

4. Put the garlic stuffed pork in the cooker

5. Sprinkle the garlic powder and salt on the pork.

6. Cover and let it cook on low heat for 9 – 10 hours.

7. Once the pork is fully cooked, shred it using two forks.

8. Melt and heat bacon fat in a skillet over medium-high heat.

9. Add the mushrooms and salt in it. Cook till the mushrooms get soft.

10. Add the remaining ingredients in the skillet and mix well.

11. Take it out on the serving tray and top it up with shredded pork. Enjoy!

Sweet Blueberry Carnitas

Serving Size

5 – 6 servings

Nutritional Facts (Values per Serving)

Calories/serving: 282

Total Carbohydrate: 17.2 g

Sodium: 433 mg

Protein: 16.3 g

Cholesterol: 47 mg

Total Fat: 7.5 g

Ingredients

3 lbs pork shoulder roast

5 strips of bacon (cooked and diced)

Half cup apple juice

2 cups blueberries

1 teaspoon dried parsley

¼ cup maple syrup

Half teaspoon dried sage

¼ teaspoon nutmeg

1 teaspoon ground cinnamon

Bacon fat to fry

Salt to taste

Black pepper to taste

Fresh parsley to garnish

Preparation Method

1. Pour the apple juice in a crock pot.
2. Put the pork roast in the pot.
3. Add the maple syrup, nutmeg, ground cinnamon, dried sage, dried parsley, salt and pepper in it. Mix well.
4. Finally add the blueberries.
5. Cover and let it cook on low heat for 8 hours.
6. Once the pork is fully cooked, shred it using 2 forks.
7. Mix half of the diced bacon in the shredded pork.
8. Heat the bacon fat in a skillet.
9. Pour the meat mixture in it and press it down with a wooden spoon. Give it the shape of a large burger patty.
10. Cook for about 4 minutes on each side. Cook more if you want to make it more crispy.
11. Take it out on the serving plate.
12. Top it up with the remaining bacon.

Garnish with chopped fresh parsley. Enjoy!

Slow Cooker Sweet Potato Soup

Serving Size

2 – 3 servings

Nutritional Facts (Values per Serving)

Calories/serving: 164

Total Carbohydrate: 17.4 g

Sodium: 43 mg

Protein: 1.6 g

Cholesterol: 0 mg

Total Fat: 9.2 g

Ingredients

2 sweet potatoes (chopped)

14oz. coconut milk

2 garlic cloves (crushed)

1 small yellow onion (sliced)

1 tablespoon dried basil

1 cup vegetable broth

Sea salt to taste

Ground black pepper to taste

Preparation Method

1. Put all the ingredients in a slow cooker. Mix well.
2. Cover and let it cook on high heat for 3 hours.
3. Pour out the content of the cooker in a food processor.
4. Blend till it becomes a smooth puree. Serve it hot!

Paleo Detox Apples

Serving Size

Makes 4 stuffed apples

Nutritional Facts (Values per Serving)

Calories/serving: 256

Total Carbohydrate: 43.4 g

Sodium: 50.2 mg

Protein: 1.2 g

Cholesterol: 15 mg

Total Fat: 11 g

Ingredients

4 green apples (cored)

2 tablespoons ground cinnamon

4 tablespoons unsweetened shredded coconut

¼ cup unsweetened sunbutter

1 cup water

Half cup melted coconut butter melted

¼ teaspoon nutmeg

¼ teaspoon salt

Preparation Method

1. In a bowl, add the sunbutter and coconut butter, nutmeg, cinnamon and salt. Mix well.
2. Put the cored apples and water in a slow cooker.
3. Stuff equal amount of butter mixture in the core of every apple.
4. Top it up with shredded coconut.

Cover and let it cook on low heat for 3 hours. Enjoy!

Asian Style Ribs

Serving Size

6 – 8 servings

Nutritional Facts (Values per Serving)

Calories/serving: 728

Total Carbohydrate: 10.6 g

Sodium: 525 mg

Protein: 33.4 g

Cholesterol: 143 mg

Total Fat: 60.1 g

Ingredients

5 lbs Grass Fed Beef Short Ribs

3 tablespoons Coconut Aminos

1 tablespoon sesame oil

1 tablespoon raw honey

1 teaspoon hot sauce

2 tablespoons white wine vinegar

2 teaspoons sesame seeds

Juice of 1 lime

2 teaspoons grated fresh ginger

Sea salt to taste

Ground black pepper to taste

Preparation Method

1. In a large bowl, mix all ingredients except for the short ribs.
2. Line the ribs in a baking tray.

3. Pour the ingredient mixture on top of it.

4. Cover the tray and put it in the refrigerator to marinate for at least 6 hours.

5. Put the ribs in a slow cooker.

6. Cover the cooker and let it cook on low heat for 7 – 8 hours. Enjoy!

Slow Cooker Barbacoa

Serving Size

3 – 4 servings

Nutritional Facts (Values per Serving)

Calories/serving: 792

Total Carbohydrate: 4.6 g

Sodium: 596 mg

Protein: 96.7 g

Cholesterol: 295 mg

Total Fat: 40.6 g

Ingredients for Roast

2 lbs. Grass Fed Beef Rump Roast

¼ cup apple cider vinegar

1 tablespoon ground cumin

¼ cup vegetable broth

7 garlic cloves

1 medium sized yellow onion (diced)

1 tablespoon chipotle peppers in adobo sauce (canned)

4 bay leaves

1 small red onion (diced)

1 cup mushrooms (chopped)

Black pepper to taste

Salt to taste

Ingredients for Sauce

16 oz. tomato sauce

1 tablespoon chipotle chili powder

1 teaspoon ground red pepper

14 oz. green chilies (canned)

Half teaspoon nutmeg

¼ teaspoon ground cloves

Half teaspoon smoked paprika

2 teaspoons cayenne pepper

Salt to taste

Black pepper to taste

Preparation Method

1. Put all the Roast ingredients in a slow cooker.
2. Mix well. Make sure the roast gets properly coated by all the ingredients.
3. Cover and let it cook on low heat for 8 hours.
4. Once the roast is fully cooked, shred the meat using two forks.
5. Add all the sauce ingredients in it.
6. Recover the cooker and let it cook on high heat for 1 hour.

The delicious Slow Cooker Barbacoa is ready to serve.

Spicy Coffee Short Ribs

Serving Size

6 – 8 servings

Nutritional Facts (Values per Serving)

Calories/serving: 833

Total Carbohydrate: 22.3 g

Sodium: 423 mg

Protein: 92.7 g

Cholesterol: 267.6 mg

Total Fat: 40.4 g

Ingredients

4 lbs. Grass Fed Beef Short Ribs

4 dried ancho chiles

1 cup brewed coffee

4 garlic cloves

1 large yellow onion (sliced)

2 tablespoons raw honey

Half cup vegetable broth

2 tablespoons extra virgin olive oil

1 tablespoon lime juice

Black pepper to taste

Salt to taste

Preparation Method

1. Remove the stems and seeds of the ancho chiles.
2. Fill a large bowl with hot water and soak the ancho chiles in it.

3. Let it sit for 30 minutes or till the chiles soften.

4. Put the softened chiles, garlic cloves, olive oil, brewed coffee, lime juice, honey, salt and pepper in a food processor.

5. Blend till it becomes a smooth puree.

6. Line a slow cooker with sliced onions.

7. Add broth on top of it.

8. Now put the ribs in the cooker.

9. Pour the blended puree on top of it.

10. Cover and cook for 8 hours on low heat. Enjoy!

Crockpot Chicken Gravy

Serving Size

3 – 4 servings

Nutritional Facts (Values per Serving)

Calories/serving: 549.3

Total Carbohydrate: 55.3 g

Sodium: 212.4 mg

Protein: 32 g

Cholesterol: 118.2 mg

Total Fat: 22.3 g

Ingredients

2 lbs. chicken breasts

2 tablespoons tomato paste

¾ cup coconut milk

3 garlic cloves (crushed)

5 tablespoons curry powder

1 cup chicken broth

1 red bell pepper (cut in 1 inch cubes)

1 yellow bell pepper (cut in 1 inch cubes)

1 tablespoon ground ginger

1 medium sized yellow onion (thinly sliced)

Pinch of crushed red pepper

Black pepper to taste

Salt to taste

Preparation Method

1. Add tomato paste, coconut milk, curry powder, ground ginger, garlic, crushed red pepper, salt and pepper in a slow cooker. Mix well.

2. Now add the bell pepper cubes, onions, chicken and broth in it. Mix well.

3. Cover and let it cook on high heat for 4 – 5 hours or on low heat for 7 – 8 hours. Enjoy!

Paleo Ropa Vieja with Rice

Serving Size

3 – 4 servings

Nutritional Facts (Values per Serving)

Calories/serving: 328

Total Carbohydrate: 29.1 g

Sodium: 1038 mg

Protein: 40.5 g

Cholesterol: 96.9 mg

Total Fat: 9.6 g

Ingredients for Vieja

2 lbs. chuck roast

1 medium sized yellow onion (sliced)

1 red bell pepper (thinly sliced)

1 yellow bell pepper (thinly sliced)

6 oz. tomato sauce

14 oz. canned diced tomatoes

3 tablespoons capers (drained)

1 tablespoon ground cumin

1 tablespoon dried thyme

1 tablespoon dried oregano

4 garlic cloves

1 bay leaf

Black pepper to taste

Salt to taste

Ingredients for rice

- 1 head of cauliflower (stems removed)
- 3 slices bacon (chopped)
- 4 oz. tomato sauce
- 2 teaspoons ground cumin
- 1 teaspoon garlic powder
- 1 teaspoon onion powder
- Black pepper to taste
- Salt to taste

Preparation Method

1. With the tip of a sharp knife, poke four holes in the chuck roast.
2. Stuff a garlic clove in every hole.
3. Line the base of a slow cooker with sliced onions and bell peppers.
4. Put the garlic-stuffed roast on top of the onions and peppers.
5. Then add the remaining Vieja ingredients in the cooker.
6. Cover and let it cook on low heat for 7 – 8 hours.
7. When the roast is fully cooked, shred the meat using 2 forks.
8. To make the rice, put the cauliflower in a food processor and chop till it becomes like rice.
9. Brown the bacon in a skillet. Then add in it the cauliflower rice. Mix well.
10. Now add rest of the rice ingredients in the saucepan. Mix well.
11. Cover the pan and let it cook on medium heat for 12 – 15 minutes. Stir once in between.
12. Pour it in a serving tray. Top it up with shredded roast and serve.

Crock Pot Roast with Mushroom Gravy

Serving Size

3 – 4 servings

Nutritional Facts (Values per Serving)

Calories/serving: 993

Total Carbohydrate: 9.8 g

Sodium: 733 mg

Protein: 64.5 g

Cholesterol: 234.7 mg

Total Fat: 77.4 g

Ingredients

2 lbs. beef rump roast

Half cup coconut milk

2 cups mushrooms (sliced)

4 cups chicken broth

1 teaspoon garlic powder

1 teaspoon onion powder

2 large onions (diced)

6 garlic cloves

Half teaspoon paprika

Black pepper to taste

Salt to taste

Preparation Method

1. Put all the ingredients in a crock pot. Mix well.
2. Cover and let it cook on low heat for 7 – 8 hours or on high heat for 5 – 6 hours.

Serve hot!

Slow Cooked Garlic Rump Roast

Serving Size

3 – 4 servings

Nutritional Facts (Values per Serving)

Calories/serving: 371

Total Carbohydrate: 9.6 g

Sodium: 175 mg

Protein: 45.1 g

Cholesterol: 145 mg

Total Fat: 17 g

Ingredients

2 lbs. pork rump roast

2 heads of cauliflower (stems removed)

6 garlic cloves

1 cup chicken broth

1 teaspoon cumin

1 teaspoon salt

Half teaspoon black pepper

Preparation Method

1. Put the cauliflower in a food processor and chop till it becomes like rice.
2. With the tip of a sharp knife, poke 3 holes in the roast.
3. Stuff a garlic clove in each hole.
4. Toss the cauliflower rice, the remaining garlic cloves and all the other ingredients in a crock pot. Mix well.
5. Put the garlic-stuffed roast on top of it.

6. Cover and let it cook on low heat for 9 – 10 hours.

7. Once the pork is fully cooked, shred it using two forks.

8. Mix it with rice and serve.

Mexican Lime Soup with Rice

Serving Size

2 – 3 servings

Nutritional Facts (Values per Serving)

Calories/serving: 484

Total Carbohydrate: 35.7 g

Sodium: 300.3 mg

Protein: 29.9 g

Cholesterol: 49.2 mg

Total Fat: 29.1 g

Ingredients for Soup

1 lb chicken breast

14 oz. canned diced tomatoes

1 tablespoon olive oil

1 medium sized yellow onion (chopped)

Half cup chicken broth

14 oz. canned roasted red peppers

1 tablespoon chili powder

1 teaspoon garlic powder

2 teaspoons ground cumin

2 garlic cloves (minced)

1 teaspoon oregano

1 teaspoon black pepper

1 teaspoon salt

Ingredients for Rice

1 head of cauliflower

4 tablespoons cilantro (chopped)

1 tablespoon olive oil

2 teaspoons lime juice

Preparation Method

1. Toss all the soup ingredients in a crock pot. Mix well.
2. Cover and let it cook on high heat for 4 hours.
3. Once the chicken is fully cooked, shred it using 2 forks. Mix it with other ingredients in the pot.
4. Next, preheat the oven to 400 degrees.
5. Remove the leaves and stems of the cauliflower and cut it into small florets.
6. Line a baking dish with cauliflower florets. Sprinkle salt and olive oil on top it.
7. Bake it for 25 – 30 minutes.
8. Once the baking is done, put the baked cauliflower florets in a food processor.
9. Chop till it takes the shape of rice.
10. In a large bowl, mix together the cauliflower rice, chopped cilantro and lime juice.
11. Take it out on the serving tray.
12. Top it up with the shredded chicken gravy. Enjoy!

Cinnamon Chops with Butternut Squash

Serving Size

Serves 2

Nutritional Facts (Values per Serving)

Calories/serving: 387

Total Carbohydrate: 16 g

Sodium: 370 mg

Protein: 24.9 g

Cholesterol: 80.4 mg

Total Fat: 26.2 g

Ingredients

2 large pork chops

1 medium sized red onion (sliced)

1 sweet onion (sliced)

2 medium sized apples (sliced)

2 tablespoons raw honey

4 tablespoons coconut oil

1 teaspoon mustard powder

2 teaspoons cinnamon powder

Black pepper to taste

Salt to taste

Ingredients for Butternut Squash

1 medium sized butternut squash

1 teaspoon cinnamon powder

1 tablespoon coconut oil

Half cup chicken broth

¼ teaspoon nutmeg

Pinch of salt

Preparation Method

1. Peel and dice the butternut squash.
2. Toss it in a slow cooker with all other butternut squash ingredients.
3. Cover and let it cook on low heat for 2 hours or on high heat for 1 hour.
4. While the chicken is cooking, heat 2 skillets over medium heat. (If you cannot manage 2 skillets at the same time, you can also perform this one by one)
5. Put half of the coconut oil in one skillet and half in the other.
6. Put the sliced onions in one skillet and sliced apples in another.
7. Stir for a while.
8. When the apples and onions become translucent, put half quantity of the honey and cinnamon powder in one skillet and half in the other. Mix well.
9. Add a pinch of salt in both skillets. Stir till the onions and apples caramelize a bit.
10. When apples and onions are caramelized, turn off the heat and pour them out in the same bowl.
11. Mix together the apples and onions and set aside.
12. Set the oven to preheat to 350 degrees.
13. Season the pork chops with cinnamon powder, salt, pepper, and mustard powder.
14. Heat a skillet and put pork chops it in (You can also use the same skillet that you used for caramelizing onions).
15. Cook for 4 – 5 minutes on both sides.
16. Line the base of a baking sheet with apple-onion mixture.
17. Put the chops on top of it.
18. Bake it for 20 – 25 minutes.
19. Once the butternut squash is cooked, mash it using a fork or potato masher.

To serve, put the mashed butternut squash in a serving tray. Top it up with chops followed by apple-onion mixture. Enjoy!

Slow Cooker Chuck Roast

Serving Size

4 – 5 servings

Nutritional Facts (Values per Serving)

Calories/serving: 352

Total Carbohydrate: 13 g

Sodium: 657 mg

Protein: 34.9 g

Cholesterol: 111.5 mg

Total Fat: 17.1 g

Ingredients

3 lbs. Chuck Roast

1 Onion (cut in large chunks)

5 medium sized Potatoes (cut in large chunks)

4 Carrots (thickly sliced)

Half teaspoon Garlic Powder

Half teaspoon Italian Seasoning

Half teaspoon Onion Powder

2 Cups Beef Stock

2 Cups Water

Pinch of Salt

Pinch of black pepper

Preparation Method

1. Put all the ingredients in a crock pot. Mix well.

2. Cover and let it cook on high heat for 5 – 6 hours. Enjoy!

Paleo Chick 'n' Basil

Serving Size

4 – 6 servings

Nutritional Facts (Values per Serving)

Calories/serving: 422

Total Carbohydrate: 22.9 g

Sodium: 565 mg

Protein: 15.5 g

Cholesterol: 85.5 mg

Total Fat: 13.2 g

Ingredients

6 chicken breasts (boneless and skinless)

1 medium sized white onion (chopped)

25 oz. tomato basil marinara sauce

4 carrots (sliced)

14 oz. canned diced tomatoes

3 cloves garlic

1 tablespoon oregano

Half cup fresh basil

Black pepper to taste

Salt to taste

Preparation Method

1. Put chicken breasts in a crock pot.
2. Add onions, carrots, garlic and diced tomatoes in it.
3. Top it up with the tomato basil marinara, oregano, salt and pepper.

4. Spread the fresh basil on top.

5. Cover and let it cook on low heat for 7 – 8 hours.

Serve over cooked rice. Enjoy!

Paleo BBQ Style Bison

Serving Size

4 – 5 servings

Nutritional Facts (Values per Serving)

Calories/serving: 299

Total Carbohydrate: 6.9 g

Sodium: 238.5 mg

Protein: 24.2 g

Cholesterol: 81 mg

Total Fat: 17 g

Ingredients

3 lbs. bison chuck roast

1 large red onion (sliced)

2 tablespoons coconut oil

1 cup water

Black pepper to taste

Salt to taste

BBQ sauce to serve

Preparation Method

1. Wash the bison roast and pat dry.
2. Rub the coconut oil over it.
3. Coat the roast with salt and pepper.
4. Line a slow cooker with sliced onion.
5. Put the roast on top of it.
6. Add water, cover and let it cook on low heat for 11 – 12 hours.

Serve it with BBQ sauce. Enjoy!

Paleo Italian Roast with Balsamic Vinegar

Serving Size

3 – 4 servings

Nutritional Facts (Values per Serving)

Calories/serving: 269.3

Total Carbohydrate: 8.6 g

Sodium: 511 mg

Protein: 33.7 g

Cholesterol: 99.7 mg

Total Fat: 10.8 g

Ingredients

2 lbs. round roast

Half cup balsamic vinegar

1 large sweet onion (sliced)

Half cup water

8 oz. tomato sauce

2 tablespoons coconut oil

2 tablespoons white wine

Spices

1 teaspoon smoked paprika

1 teaspoon onion powder

1 teaspoon garlic powder

Salt to taste

Black Pepper to taste

Preparation Method

1. Season the roast with spices.
2. Heat coconut oil in a large skillet over medium heat.
3. Put the roast in the skillet and cook for 4 – 5 minutes on each side.
4. Line the bottom of a crock pot with sliced onions.
5. Put the seared roast on top of it.
6. In another bowl, mix together the balsamic vinegar and tomato sauce. Pour it on top of the roast.
7. In another saucepan, de-glaze the white wine and water for a while. Pour it in the crock pot.
8. Cover and let it cook on low heat for 7 – 8 hours. Enjoy!

Slow Cooker Meat Fajitas

Serving Size

2 – 3 servings

Nutritional Facts (Values per Serving)

Calories/serving: 301.3

Total Carbohydrate: 23.5 g

Sodium: 302.8 mg

Protein: 33 g

Cholesterol: 39 mg

Total Fat: 8.8 g

Ingredients

2 lbs. flank steak

2 jalapenos (seeded and chopped)

1 large onion (diced)

1 red bell pepper (seeded and diced)

1 yellow bell pepper (seeded and diced)

Spices

1 teaspoon ground cumin

2 teaspoons chili powder

¼ teaspoon onion powder

¼ teaspoon garlic powder

Pinch of cayenne pepper

Half teaspoon black pepper

1 teaspoon salt

Fresh cilantro to garnish

Preparation Method

1. Mix all the spices and coat the mixture on both sides of the steak.
2. Put the seasoned beef in a slow cooker.
3. Add the diced onions and bell peppers in the cooker.
4. Cover and let it cook on low heat for 9 – 10 hours.
5. Once the beef is fully cooked, shred it using 2 forks and mix it with all other ingredients in the cooker.

Garnish with chopped fresh cilantro. Enjoy!

Sweet and Hearty Lasagna

Serving Size

10 – 12 servings

Nutritional Facts (Values per Serving)

Calories/serving: 533

Total Carbohydrate: 62.8 g

Sodium: 1178 mg

Protein: 35 g

Cholesterol: 96 mg

Total Fat: 18.7 g

Ingredients

10 ounces frozen spinach

12 ounces mozzarella cheese (shredded)

12 ounces sweet potato (peeled and thinly sliced)

5 ounces ricotta cheese

Pinch of nutmeg

Half teaspoon salt

Fresh Parsley to garnish

Grated parmesan cheese to garnish

Ingredients for Sauce

1 lb ground meat (chicken, beef or turkey)

6 ounces tomato paste

3 cups crushed tomato

1 medium sized onion (chopped)

1 tablespoon oregano

1 tablespoon dried parsley

4 teaspoons dried basil

4 teaspoons garlic powder

4 teaspoons onion powder

2 teaspoons dried thyme

1 teaspoon black pepper

2 teaspoons salt

¼ teaspoon crushed red pepper

Preparation Method

1. Brown the ground meat in a skillet.
2. Add all the sauce ingredients in it. Mix well and set aside.
3. Thaw and drain the frozen spinach.
4. Add ricotta, salt, spinach and nutmeg in a food processor. Blend well.
5. In a slow cooker, layer the ingredients in the following sequence.

One-third of the meat sauce – Half of the sweet potato slices – half of the blended spinach mixture – One-third of the mozzarella cheese – Repeat the layer.

6. Top up the second layer with the remaining meat sauce and mozzarella cheese.
7. Cover and let it cook on low heat for 6 hours or on high heat for 3 hours.

Garnish with grated parmesan cheese and chopped cilantro. Enjoy!

Crockpot Saffron Meat

Serving Size

6 – 8 servings

Nutritional Facts (Values per Serving)

Calories/serving: 528.3

Total Carbohydrate: 8.8 g

Sodium: 1231 mg

Protein: 44.2 g

Cholesterol: 151 mg

Total Fat: 34.5 g

Ingredients

4 lbs. boneless pork (cut into 4 equal pieces)

1 big red onion (cut into 4 quarters)

5 garlic cloves (crushed)

28 ounces canned diced tomatoes

1 tablespoon fresh chives

Half teaspoon Saffron

2 tablespoons cooking fat

1 tablespoon fresh parsley

¼ cup Hot Water

Salt to taste

Spices

1 teaspoon oregano

1 tablespoon Spanish paprika

1 teaspoon cilantro

Half tablespoon ground cumin

1 teaspoon crushed red pepper

Ingredients for Sauce

2 tablespoons olive oil

1 tablespoon arrowroot starch

¼ cup full fat coconut milk

Preparation Method

1. Crush the saffron and mix it with hot water. Set aside.
2. Mix all the spices in a bowl and set aside.
3. Heat the cooking fat in a pan over medium heat.
4. Brown the pork in it. Sear for 4 – 5 minutes on each side.
5. Put the seared pork in a slow cooker. Leave the cooking fat behind in the pan.
6. Add the onion, spice mixture and garlic in the same pan.
7. Cook till the onions are translucent.
8. Pour out the contents of the pan in the slow cooker.
9. In the same pan, slightly de-glaze the tomatoes and then add them in the cooker.
10. Finally, add the saffron water, parsley and chives in the slow cooker. Mix well.
11. Cover and let it cook on low heat for 7 – 8 hours.
12. When the chicken is half way cooked, take out 1 cup of broth from it to make the sauce.
13. To make the sauce, mix together the broth, olive oil and coconut milk in a saucepan.
14. Let it simmer on medium heat for 6 – 7 minutes.
15. Turn off the heat.
16. Add the arrowroot starch in it and mix till it is completely dissolved.

Serve the sauce separately or serve it over the pork. It is up to you. Enjoy!

Smokey Pork with BBQ Sauce

Serving Size

3 – 4 servings

Nutritional Facts (Values per Serving)

Calories/serving: 532.9

Total Carbohydrate: 56.2 g

Sodium: 834 mg

Protein: 44.2 g

Cholesterol: 31 mg

Total Fat: 22.4 g

Ingredients for BBQ Spice Blend

2 tablespoons sweet paprika

2 teaspoons garlic powder

2 tablespoons smoked paprika

1 tablespoon celery seed

2 teaspoons salt

1 tablespoon chili powder

Half tablespoon rubbed Dalmation sage

1 teaspoon onion powder

Half tablespoon black pepper

1 teaspoons allspice

¼ teaspoon cayenne pepper

½ teaspoon cumin

½ teaspoon bay leaf

¼ teaspoon mace

¼ teaspoon cloves

Ingredients for Sweet BBQ Sauce

> 3 tablespoons blackstrap molasses
>
> Half tablespoon Dijon mustard
>
> Half cup apple cider vinegar
>
> 2 tablespoons Coconut Aminos
>
> 3 tablespoons raw honey
>
> 6 ounces tomato paste
>
> 8 ounces tomato sauce
>
> 2 tablespoons BBQ spice blend (ingredients above)

Ingredients for Pork

> 2 lbs. pork shoulder (cut into approximately 3 inch pieces)
>
> 3 cups chicken broth
>
> 1 tablespoon Muscovado sugar
>
> 1 big yellow onion (sliced)
>
> 1 cup Sweet BBQ Sauce (ingredients above)
>
> ¼ cup BBQ Spice Blend (ingredients above)

Preparation Method

1. **To make the BBQ spice blend,** add all the BBQ spice blend ingredients in a food processor.
2. Run the processor for a few minutes to mix well all the ingredients.
3. **To make the sweet BBQ sauce**, add all the sweet BBQ sauce ingredients in a saucepan.
4. Bring it to a boil.
5. Let it simmer on low heat for 30 minutes while stirring occasionally.
6. Now that the sauces are ready, let's move on to the pork.

7. Mix together the BBQ spice blend and sugar in a large bowl.

8. Put the pork pieces in the bowl and coat this mixture on them.

9. Cover the bowl and put it in the refrigerator to marinate for 2 hours.

10. Line the bottom of a crock pot with sliced onion.

11. Put the marinated pork on top of the onions.

12. Pour chicken broth in the pot.

13. Cover and let it cook on low heat for 9 – 10 hours.

14. Once the pork is fully cooked, shred it using two forks.

15. Mix in it the sweet BBQ sauce.

16. Cover and let it cook on low heat for another 2 hours.

The delectable Smokey pork with BBQ sauce is ready to serve.

Vegan Minestrone Soup

Serving Size

6 – 8 servings

Nutritional Facts (Values per Serving)

Calories/serving: 173

Total Carbohydrate: 28.5 g

Sodium: 577.7 mg

Protein: 6.8 g

Cholesterol: 4.5 mg

Total Fat: 4.3 g

Ingredients

2 tablespoons olive oil

2 celery stalks (thickly chopped)

1 medium sized sweet potato (sliced)

2 zucchini squash (diced)

1 cup sliced carrot

28 ounces vegetable broth

2 shallots (thickly chopped)

1 cup fresh spinach (diced)

2 garlic cloves (crushed)

28 ounces canned diced tomatoes

2 bay leaves

1 teaspoons parsley

2 teaspoons oregano

1 teaspoons basil

¼ teaspoon cayenne pepper

¼ teaspoon sea salt

Preparation Method

1. Put olive oil, carrots, sweet potatoes, zucchini, celery, shallots and garlic in a slow cooker. Mix well.
2. Add all the remaining ingredients in the cooker. Put bay leaves on top.
3. Cover and let it cook on low heat for 7 – 8 hours.

Discard bay leaves before serving. Enjoy!

Final Words

So how many recipes did you try so far? By now you must have gotten an idea on how comprehensive this recipe book is. With 75 recipes, this book will make you an expert on Paleo slow cooker recipes.

Paleo is healthy! This combined with the fact that slow cooker food is easy to make with most of the recipes just asking you to dump all ingredients in the crock pot and then forget it for a couple of hours, makes Paleo slow cooker recipes highly convenient in today's busy era.

Well, keep on trying these recipes and forget the hassles of cooking.

Good Luck!!